banana boys

Banana Boys

The Play

By Leon Aureus
Adapted from the
Novel by Terry Woo

Playwrights Canada Press
Toronto • Canada

PLAYWRIGHTS CANADA PRESS
215 Spadina Avenue, Suite 230, Toronto, Ontario, Canada M5T 2C7
phone 416.703.0013 fax 416.408.3402
info@playwrightscanada.com • www.playwrightscanada.com

Playwrights Canada Press acknowledges the financial support of the Government
of Canada through the Canada Book Fund and the Canada Council for the Arts
and of the Province of Ontario through the Ontario Arts Council and the
Ontario Media Development Corporation for our publishing activities.

Front cover photos by Guy Bertrand. *l to r:* Derek Kwan, Richard Lee, Insurp Choi, Dale
Yim, David Yee. Cover design by Leon Aureus.
Production Editor: JLArt

LIBRARY AND ARCHIVES CANADA CATALOGUING IN PUBLICATION

Aureus, Leon, 1973-
    Banana boys : the play / by Leon Aureus ; adapted from the novel
by Terry Woo.

ISBN 978-0-88754-516-0

    1. Chinese Canadians--Drama. I. Title.

PS8601.U78B35 2007   C812'.6   C2007-900385-0

First edition: April 2007. Third printing: January 2012.
Printed and bound in Canada by Gauvin Press, Gatineau.

For my family

and for the fu-ture GENeration...

"There's a place for us out there. I know it.
And if there isn't, we'll damn well make one."
[from Terry Woo's novel, *Banana Boys*
the quote that started this all for me...]

Table of Contents

Banana Boys: The End of the Beginning
by Terry Watada

As I watched the premiere performance of the fu-GEN Asian Canadian Theatre Company's production of *Banana Boys* in September 2004, I found it to be a revelation. The dynamic cast of Insurp Choi, Derek Kwan, Richard Lee, David Yee and Dale Yim was impressive. Each actor imbued his role with compassion, love, anger, humour and hope, which went well beyond caricature and stereotype, the traditional fate of Asian characters. Nina Lee Aquino's direction was assured, creating a production that was innovative and highly theatrical. The production team of Camellia Koo, Romeo Candido, Michelle Ramsay and Guy Bertrand had obviously worked hard and in concert to craft a polished result. Above all, Leon Aureus as playwright was able to delve into the depths of the novel by Terry Woo to go beyond the mere retelling of the story in order to make astute observations on the human experience. To my mind, what appeared before me was in fact the culmination of nearly twenty years of struggle to establish an Asian-Canadian theatre.

Olivia Chow, former Toronto city councillor and currently Member of Parliament, sat with me that evening. We joked in the way old friends do about our reasons for being there. "Got to support Asians, right?" we concluded. We had been doing just that since the early 1980s when she was learning the ropes from Dan Heap and I was looking for a way to go after several years of writing, recording and touring my music. In 1983, a few friends and I founded the Canasian Artists Group, a broad-based arts organization whose mandate was to promote Asian Canadians. Our first project was a production of *Yellow Fever*, a play highly successful in America and written by Japanese Canadian Rick Shiomi. Thus began Asian-Canadian theatre.

We lasted two productions and then I foolishly ventured out on my own (also with a few friends). After *Song for a Nisei Fisherman*, however, I had had enough. The problems seemed insurmountable. Although the mainstream press was rooting for us, the Asian communities were not – it was as if it was incumbent on us to teach Asians to go to the theatre and to appreciate our efforts. How, was the question.

In the fifteen years since then, wholly Asian-Canadian companies and productions came and went with really no cohesion, no ideological centre. I wrote a couple of plays with Asian-Canadian themes but in both cases

I was commissioned to produce something for a specific festival. But then fu-GEN came along.

Nina Lee Aquino one day contacted me when she was a grad student at the University of Toronto because she and a classmate were doing a presentation on Asian-Canadian theatre. I was impressed that she even knew I had done anything. We met in a downtown restaurant (the first of many) and I was taken with her enthusiasm and knowledge. She certainly had done her homework. She bemoaned the fact that there was no Asian-Canadian theatre, in effect there were precious few places for her to develop her talents. I could only agree.

It was perhaps a year later that she called again to arrange a meeting for her friends and me. We met and I was greeted by a group of very respectful, intelligent and young individuals: besides Nina, Richard Lee, David Yee and Leon Aureus showed up for coffee and conversation. They were exploring ways and means of starting an Asian-Canadian theatre company. I was seen as someone with some experience in that area.

I certainly didn't want to discourage them, but I didn't hold back on what they were up against: lack of money, indifference from their own communities and actor egos to name a few. But no matter what horrifying anecdotes I came up with, I could see I wasn't going to dampen their spirits. They were truly remarkable, committed and persistent artists.

I was later impressed by their ability to attract a crowd. Whether it be a showcase reading of play scenes, a public reading of a play, or a playwright's potluck, the room was always full, mostly Asian Canadians to boot. It seemed the next generation was ready to establish a voice in the mainstream and was willing to support the effort.

I was further impressed with their professionalism. I was very lucky to have them help me develop my one-act *Tale of a Mask* into a full-length play. Throughout the multi-day workshop, I was put through my paces. Nina, through gentle and constructive criticism, pointed out the possibilities for the work. The actors gave their all in lifting the words off the page. And the redoubtable Richard Lee choreographed the fight scenes with grace and excitement. In the end, I came away with a solid production-ready script.

If I had any concerns about this fledgling group it was finding out their particular vision of Asian-Canadian theatre. Many who came before had no clue or presented Asian-themed plays but with no Asian (Canadian or otherwise) input whatsoever. One prominent Japanese organization in fact could not see why any "Canadian" would want to pay to watch Asian-Canadian actors on stage. I had nothing to fear as it turned out. With an abiding affection for the past and a deep appreciation for what was happening in the present, fu-GEN strives to bring and nurture Asian-Canadian voices to Canadian theatre with whatever themes or issues they want to explore.

Banana Boys is the quintessential example of such. It contains the voices of thirty-something Asian-Canadians seeking a place in the world, and audience members like my twelve-year-old son whom I took to the Factory Theatre production are listening. I was gratified to learn that my son saw David Yee's character, Dave Lowe, as something of a hero.

So *Banana Boys* and fu-GEN are the end of the beginning of Asian-Canadian theatre. With remounts in Toronto, Ottawa and Vancouver, an advantageous relationship with Factory Theatre established and *Singkil*, their second production about to make its debut, fu-GEN has a rosy future. I am confident they will take their foothold and shepherd Asian-Canadian theatre through to its maturity. I'm sure Olivia and I and many more like us are looking forward to that eventuality.

December 2006

Acknowledgements

The playwright would like to acknowledge: Nina Lee Aquino and the original "B-Boys," Terry Woo, Camellia Koo, Michelle Ramsay, Romeo Candido, Guy Bertrand, Isaac Thomas and Jennifer Lau who have all been vital to the development of this play.

Special acknowledgment to David Yee, for his invaluable ideas, input, and dramaturgical support.

Also thanks to Daniel Christopher Chen, Silver Kim, Tim Hamaguchi, Kent Lam, Olaf Sham, Norman Yeung, Yee Jee Tso, Mary Vingoe, Terry Watada, Ken Gass and Factory Theatre, Yvette Nolan, Philip Adams, Jennifer Yap, Leanne Poon, Aaron Kelly, James Wilson, Jean Yoon, the Laidlaw Foundation, the Toronto Arts Council, the Ontario Arts Council, the Canada Council for the Arts, and the Hastings Park Foundation.

And finally, thank-you to family & friends for their understanding and love during the most insane love/hate bout of artistic creation in the short history of us.

The world premiere of *Banana Boys* was produced by fu-GEN Asian-Canadian Theatre Company in association with Factory Theatre at the Factory Studio Theatre in September 2004, with the following company:

Luke Yeung	Insurp Choi
Michael Chao	Derek Kwan
Rick Wong	Richard Lee
Dave Lowe	David Yee
Sheldon Kwan	Dale Yim

Director and Dramaturge: Nina Lee Aquino
Assistant Dramaturge: David Yee
Set and Costume Designer: Camellia Koo
Music and Sound Designer: Romeo Candido
Lighting Designer: Michelle Ramsay
Multimedia Designer: Guy Bertrand
Fight Director: Richard Lee
Movement Coach: Catherine Hernandez
Stage Manager: Isaac Thomas
Apprentice Stage Manager: Jennifer Lau

• • •

Banana Boys was commissioned, developed and workshopped by fu-GEN Asian-Canadian Theatre Company in 2002. It was presented as a staged reading on July 10, 2003 at Tallulah's Cabaret, Buddies in Bad Times Theatre with the above-mentioned actors and Nina Lee Aquino as Director and Dramaturge.

• • •

In a revised text, the play was subsequently toured by fu-GEN Asian-Canadian Theatre Company to the 2005 Magnetic North Theatre Festival in Ottawa with the same company and the following additional credits:
Associate Sound Designer   Richard Lee
Multimedia Co-Designer   Leon Aureus

• • •

Banana Boys was then remounted with another revised text by fu-GEN Asian-Canadian Theatre Company and Factory Theatre in September 2005 at the Factory Studio Theatre with the same company.

• • •

This published text includes sections rewritten since the Factory Theatre remount.

Characters

Luke Yeung
Michael Chao
Rick Wong
Dave Lowe
Sheldon Kwan

Note: Other characters appear intermittently at the Director's discretion.

Banana Boys

Prologue

> *Complete darkness. The sound of wind chimes. A soft*
> *pale light, the shape of a full moon goes up on a screen.*
> *A woman's voice, ghostly and haunting is heard in the*
> *darkness, far away at first but soon grows in volume.*

VOICE   Wo ei ni, wo ei ni, wo ei ni...

> *A soft peal of bells. A few seconds later it is followed*
> *by the sound of shattering glass. Almost imperceptibly,*
> *a man moans in pain.*

Wo ei ni... *(pause)* ...I love you.

> *Shift.*

> *RICK is lying in his coffin, a large triangle of mirrored*
> *glass sticking out of his chest. It is his funeral.*

RICK   I'm mindshifting into the future. It's a thing I do. Like
most things I do, I've become remarkably good at it. It is,
I think, the key to my success. I see things before they
happen. I know things before they are conceived of in
the meager imagination of "the other guy." I am fully,
entirely, completely, unequivocally... aware. I achieve
this by a combination of sheer willpower, mental
conditioning and God-given talent. *(pause)* The drugs
and alcohol help too.

I've found that by mindshifting into the future, I have
a greater control over what occurs in the present, and an
even greater understanding of what has transpired in the
past. *(Pause. He tries to move the glass in his chest. It won't
budge.)* Of course, there are a few exceptions, we all have
our off days. Take, for example, the large mirror they
found in my chest. *(pause)* Hurt like a motherfucker. But
I feel no pain. I'm in the future. All the pain is in the
present, and I've escaped it by mindshifting forward.

In the future, I'm... at my funeral. An event likely tied to the large mirror in my chest. *(beat)* Mike always said self-image would be the death of me. *(He laughs, but coughs up blood.)* Nasty business, that. *(cheerier)* Tasmin's here. Sexy even in mourning. Crying, wailing like a banshee. I made her wail like that a few times, it's kinda turning me on. Mom and Dad, all morose and solemn. *(yells at them)* C'mon pussies! Have a drink, liven up a little! *(He laughs and coughs up more blood.)* Nasty business. *(He surveys the room.)* I wonder...

Hey, Shirl's here. The whole family, together again. Nuclear us. Hey Shirl! Shirl! God, look sad or something, ice queen, your fuckin' brother's dead. *(pause)* Bitch.

Where are the... did they...

Y'know... I've slept with over 60% of the women in here. Some of them at the same time. The look on their faces when they find out—

> *Pause.*

Wait.

> *He fast forwards.*

No one finds out? No one... no one ever knows? Conquests: Physical and Financial. Perfectly executed plans for World Domination. I didn't... how are they going to know how great I was if.... This has to change. I need...

...my emergency recorder, my black box, where the fuck is...?

> *MIKE enters.*

Heh. And so it begins...

ACT ONE: THE BOOK™: In which they are revealed

Scene One

MIKE enters. He stands, unmoving. His heart is filled with static; electric snow. He does not speak. The air is filled with thick, muddy white noise. He stands like this, morose, for a 23-year-old.

Finally, a Campbell's soup box appears at his feet. The noise begins to fade. The static shrinks into his heart, revealing it.

He is saved.

MIKE   Mental White Noise. The purposeless introspection that intrudes on your train of thought when you should be thinking about school, laundry, or paying your electric bill. Mental White Noise is directionless, keeps you from the important things in life. Like a daydream on downers. Daydreams are generally pleasant. Mental White Noise is controlling and obsessive and completely unavoidable. Like boy bands, but malicious. And I'm tired of it. I'm tired of my energy being wasted thinking about what should'a been, could'a been, women, school, grades, The Book. I want to focus. Pay attention. *(to himself)* You're not paying attention. *(beat)* Focus. On what's really important. *(pause)* Med School. *(He coughs.)* Med School. *(He coughs.)* Med... *(He waits. Nothing. He presumes it is safe.)* ...School— *(He coughs. Pause. He is sullen.)* The only answer, as far as I can figure it... is electroconvulsive shock therapy.

He is at the Second Cup coffee shop.

SERVER   I'm sorry?

MIKE   Electroconvulsive shock therapy.

SERVER   We don't serve that here.

MIKE sighs.

MIKE   Fine.

SERVER   So... what would you like?

MIKE   I... I don't know.

Scene Two

DAVE is at the supermarket. He is picking up random items, when he passes by an old Chinese WOMAN speaking to a young White CLERK.

WOMAN   Weh, bok choy hai been ah? Bok choy ah!

CLERK   What the hell is *back chewy*?

WOMAN   Bok choy ah. Chai-neez wedgie-ta-boh ah!

CLERK   I'm soll-ee, what is that?

WOMAN   Bok—

CLERK   Back?

WOMAN   Bok—

CLERK   "Wok with Yan?"

WOMAN   Bok—

CLERK   Bok Bok? Make chicken stir fry? Number 42 with pineapple?

WOMAN   Bok choy...

CLERK   Me love you long time? GI Numbah One? Give boom boom, fie dolla?

DAVE, livid, steps in.

DAVE   Excuse me. Bok choy... hai... hai... joah ah! Joah, bak choi hei joah, hai goah doh ah! [It's... it's... left! Left, the bok choi is left, over there.]

WOMAN   *Lay dee gong doong wah ho cha ah!* [Your Cantonese sucks!]

DAVE   Lady, don't I know it.

The WOMAN goes off to get her bok choy. DAVE stares down the CLERK.

	Hi there.
CLERK	Hi.
DAVE	I was wondering if you could help me. Where do you stock your crackers?
CLERK	What?
DAVE	Your crackers. Where can I find your *crackers*?
CLERK	Aisle five.
DAVE	So we must be in aisle five.
CLERK	You got a problem, buddy?
DAVE	Just with the way you harass old ladies.
CLERK	I didn't harass nobody. And it's none of your fuckin' business.
DAVE	Oh it's my business, 'cause I'm making it my business.
CLERK	*(laughs)* Like I'm really scared of you, buddy.

The CLERK tries to move past DAVE. DAVE blocks his way.

DAVE   Look, I understand. I do. I'm not much of a threat to you, standing here, in front of all these people. I'm not physically intimidating to you, so you'll brush me off and file me away as just another immigrant that got in the way of fulfilling your duties as Head Stockboy. By lunchtime, I'll be nothing but an afterthought, and by the time you go home I'll be completely erased from your underdeveloped, likely drug-addled brain. But you're forgetting one thing, buddy. I'm Chinese. And we have something called "tenacity." And what "tenacity" means is that weeks, months, maybe years from now, after a hard day's work of mocking Chinese people, I will find you. I will find you where you sleep. I will find you with the memory of this day clearly ingrained in my mind, and I will rip your fucking arms off and shove them down your throat, White boy. So you go now. You go back to your minimum-wage job and your pathetic life, and just remember what I said.

DAVE turns, without waiting for a response, and leaves the store. Outside, he leans against a wall, still livid.

DAVE's Internal Racial Log appears from his head:

Racial Incident Log. Incident: #894.

Date: November 7th.

Notes: Fair comeback. Idle threats made. Decent but unclever use of swear words. Nagging, possibly incorrect usage of word "tenacity." Felt queasy and uncomfortable afterwards, but suppressed desire to inflict bodily harm.

Grade: B-.

Comments: Good job, soldier! For that, you get a Coke!

DAVE cracks open a Coke, and drinks it, still unsettled.

Scene Three

RICK is at his end-of-quarter meeting at Jones & Lavoie. JOHN Forsyth, Senior Partner, is announcing RICK's promotion.

JOHN   I would like to announce Richard Wong's promotion to Senior Consultant. Richard's numbers are not only impressive, they are the *highest* numbers in the firm. Ladies and gentlemen, Richard T. Wong.

RICK takes the spotlight. He speaks in a mildly affected FOB (fresh off the boat) accent.

RICK   Thanks John. He's got a shitty drive, but his numbers rock. *(Everyone laughs good-naturedly.)* I'd like to thank everyone at Jones & Lavoie for making me feel welcome here, I couldn't have achieved this success without your help. If I didn't have your shoulders to stand on, I could never have beaten you to the top. My condolences to Michael Lao, who… *(He begins to mindshift. He gradually loses his FOB accent during this.)* …will be fired after today's session. You'll bounce back, Michael. Ernst & Young will take you on in another 6 months. But five years from now, you'll be found dead in your home gym, under the Nautilus machine, after trying to bench 300 lbs. You should've laid off the steroids, Mike. God help you.

> *Shift.*

Baseline Video 13. Status: Three weeks out of Jones & Lavoie. New office should be ready Thursday. Status with Tasmin: Strained because of the travelling. Jewellery should solve that. Status with The Boys: Terminated like Schwarzenegger.

> *Shift. He snaps out of it.*

What the fuck am I doing?

> *An image of the Ching-Shih, a female vampire with black eyes and thin, blood red, lips flashes across JOHN Forsyth's face. RICK recoils in horror.*

What was that? Did anyone… what the fuck was that?

> *RICK becomes more lucid, realizing he is still at his meeting.*

Heh. *(The FOB accent has returned.)* You'll have to excuse me. I'm not really feeling myself today.

> *He takes out a sheet of paper from his pocket and unfolds it. It reads:*

Name: Richard (Rick) Wong. **Age:** 26.

Occupation: Consultant, Jones & Lavoie International.

Location: Toronto (formerly New York).

Notes: Due for a promotion.

> *Now more composed, he continues.*

You can expect bigger and better things in the coming quarter. A number of you have looked at my numbers and asked me "how do you do it?" How does someone so young build such an empire? I tell you the answer is easy: Time Machine.

> *People laugh uncomfortably. RICK smiles. He is back.*

Scene Four

LUKE is at the radio station.

LUKE

Luke Yeung here, but you can call me The Yeungster. I'm the new host of the "Morning Mosh" here on CMSH radio. It's 6am, the first day of spring, and my first day here at the station. It's going pretty good, thanks for asking. No fuck-ups yet. *(pause)* Aside from just saying "fuck-up" live on the air. *(pause)* Twice. *(pause)* How 'bout some music?! *(He gives an enthusiastic "thumbs up" to the control booth.)*

Shift.

It's 6am, and blah blah blah, you know the drill. I'm here, you're there, nothing changes... you're probably on your way to some cubicle job working for some faceless corporation, just running out the clock until you go home to a loveless marriage and kids that hate you and... what's the point? *(pause)* And now for today's weather... *(He gives a casual "thumbs up" to the control booth.)*

Shift.

It's 6am, and The Yeungster's seeing you through the morning drive on this cold, wet, gruesome, glum, tired, depraved fall day. *(pause)* I think I just depressed myself. *(beat)* It's my first day back here, after "the incident" and I'm feeling much better. First off, I'd like to apologize to the listeners who witnessed my teeny-tiny breakdown on the air last month. *(pause)* See, it's not that I can't commit, it's just... how do I know she's the right one? What if, y'know, something goes wrong and then you have no exit plan, *always have an exit plan! (beat)* I know you're listening Tina. I'm sorry, okay, I'm— *(beat)* Fuck it. I don't know... here's some music. *(He gives a weak "thumbs up" to the control booth.)*

Shift.

It's 6am, the "Morning Mosh"... and the Yeungster's final hour. That's right, cool cats, *apparently* you can't speak your mind on the airwaves anymore without consequences. Especially if speaking your mind involves calling your boss a "fucking psycho" on the air.

Now, I'm just supposed to go about my day quietly and not make any noise… *(beat)* But what have I always told you, listener? Hm? *Always have an exit plan.* So, CMSH might be broadcasting some weird fucking shit for a half hour or so, as Luke Yeung signs off the air for good.

He loads a CD into the player.

So here's Pat Boone's classic "Moody River." On repeat.

He pours his coffee on the sound board.

With no way to turn it off.

He gives an emphatic middle finger to the control booth. He stalks off.

Scene Five

University of Waterloo dormitory. MIKE is sleeping. RICK enters MIKE's room.

RICK   Mike. Mike, wake up!

MIKE   *(asleep)* The Twinkies are on fire.

RICK   Mike, it's Rick.

MIKE   *(still asleep)* Shel, no. What if they find out?

RICK   Mike. *Wake up!*

           MIKE sits bolt upright.

MIKE   I didn't do it! *(He rubs his eyes.)* Mom? *(He rubs his eyes again.)* Rick?

RICK   Mike, I gotta ask you a favour.

MIKE   No problem, she told us all she was 18. Honest mistake. Can I go back to bed now?

RICK   You gotta help me, Mike. I need you to keep track of me.

MIKE   What? Keep… how?

l to r: David Yee, Richard Lee
photo by Guy Bertrand

RICK	I'm mindshifting into the future, Mike. I've reached a new level of consciousness. I can mindshift out of my present consciousness and into my future one.
MIKE	Are you drunk?
RICK	A little. Look, I need you to keep track of me at certain points in my life. Keep track of where I am, how old I am, what my status is – school, job, finances. Partners, friends. Enemies.
MIKE	Enemies?
RICK	These mindshifts never last longer than an hour or so. I need all this information to find my bearings, to seek out information about my successes and mistakes and use them in the present.
MIKE	Rick. How many pills did you take today?

RICK   I need you to do this for me, Mike. Will you? It'd mean a lot to me. Mike, you're the only one I trust. Help me. Please.

MIKE   Yah, I don't know. Sure, Rick. Just go to sleep. We'll talk about it in the morning.

RICK   I might come back to you again. Before this, after this, I'll ask you for updates. I don't know if I can mindshift backwards yet. Not useful, but might be fun.

MIKE   Sure, Rick. Whatever you say.

RICK   You really are the best, Mike. Thanks.

> *RICK leaves. A pill bottle falls out of his pocket as he goes. MIKE is about to call after him, but reconsiders. He picks up the pill bottle, opens one of his textbooks, and starts reading.*

Scene Six

SHEL is staring at his cell phone.

SHEL   Okay, cell phone, me and you need to talk. We've been through a lot together. The last 6 months here have been… marginal. I've given your number to a few people, and so far, no one calls you but The Boys back home. This sucks for both of us. I mean, we came to Ottawa to find someone. To end The Quest. Twenty-four years old, and I still hadn't had a serious girlfriend. Or any sort of girlfriend. I almost had you disconnected. *(pause)* Don't look at me like that, I didn't go through with it. And do you know why? Because the day we stopped looking… was the day we met *Her*. I went twenty minutes out of my way, in minus-thirty-degree weather, to walk Her home, breaking the ice in front of Her with my CSA approved boots so She wouldn't slip and fall. She's wonderful. *(He beams.)* I gave Her your number, and She said She'd call. So… cell phone, if ever you were going to ring, if ever you were going to make that special connection… let it be now. You're fully charged. We're sitting in the bathtub where you get the best reception. So… ring. *(It doesn't ring.)* C'mon. Please? *(nothing)* She's really special. She's got these beautiful eyes, and really great hair, and… I'm prattling, but… the way She—

> *The phone rings. SHEL is startled, then fumbles the phone and picks it up.*

Hello? *(pause)* Kathy! Hi! *(pause)* No, I'm not busy, just… waiting… for you. *(pause)* Oh man, that sounds lame, doesn't it? I didn't… uh… *(pause)* Really? Well, I think you're sweet too…

Scene Seven

> *MIKE is sleeping. He is awakened by a voice calling his name.*

VOICE   Paging Dr. Chao. Paging Dr. Michael Chao.

MIKE   Go away…

VOICE   Dr. Chao, shall I prep you for surgery?

MIKE   I'm sleeping!

VOICE   No time for sleeping, Doctor. You need surgery, now.

MIKE   Me? I need… what?

> *LUKE, DAVE and SHEL appear in scrubs, and begin prepping MIKE as the patient.*

No, no, this is wrong. *I'm* not the patient.

> *RICK enters, his scrubs stained with blood. He greets the others.*

RICK   Doctor.

LUKE   Doctor.

RICK   Doctor.

SHEL   Doctor.

RICK   Doctor.

back: Richard Lee, *on gurney:* Derek Kwan
front l to r: Dale Yim, Insurp Choi, David Yee
photo by Guy Bertrand

DAVE	Doctor.
RICK	What's the situation?
LUKE	Heart attack, Dr. Wong.
RICK	This is Dr. Chao, world renowned brain doctor.
SHEL	It's a real tragedy.
RICK	Right, let's get to it. 50ccs of sodium hypochlorite.
MIKE	Sodium... that's drain cleaner! Don't put that in me!

> *DAVE hands RICK a syringe. RICK plunges it into MIKE's arm. MIKE passes out.*

RICK	100ccs of Pyloxidin.

> *DAVE hands him another syringe. RICK plunges it into his own arm.*

Yah baby! Okay, let's cut him open.

> *The other boys take turns with scissors, scalpels and steak knives, cutting MIKE open.*

LUKE   Look at all this useless junk.

RICK   Inventory.

> *The Boys pull out random items from MIKE's chest. As they pull them out, they sound off.*

SHEL   *Catcher in the Rye*, 3rd edition.

LUKE   Michael Bublé CD.

DAVE   Sea Monkeys.

SHEL   Postcard.

RICK   From where?

SHEL   *(reading)* The edge.

LUKE   *Playboy*, 1998.

DAVE   Playmate?

LUKE   Pam Anderson.

DAVE   I'll take that. *(He pockets it.)*

SHEL   Second Cup travel mug.

LUKE   License Plate: AHKL 439.

DAVE   Transformer.

RICK   Which one?

DAVE   Bumblebee.

LUKE   If you find Optimus Prime, I got dibs.

RICK   Gentlemen!

ALL   Ye-eee-es!

> *RICK roots around MIKE's chest. It is now almost empty.*

RICK   I think I've found the root of the problem.

ALL   Yes?

RICK	This man has no heart.
	Gasps all around.
	Where his heart should be… he's got this.
	RICK pulls out a large book from MIKE's chest. He reads the title.
	The Book. (beat) Obvious title.
LUKE	Is there anything we can do for him?
RICK	I'm afraid not, doctors. Call it.
DAVE	Time of death: Early.
RICK	Can't save 'em all. *(pause)* Let's get drunk.
	They all cheer.
	MIKE wakes up with a start, screaming. The Boys have disappeared. He is alone. He breathes a sigh of relief.
MOM	Mikoh! Come get some oranges. They help you study for Mikat test!
MIKE	MCATs Mom, it's the MCATs!
	MIKE goes back to sleep. Suddenly, the image of RICK's blood-covered body, cold dead eyes staring forward, flashes all around him. RICK comes up from behind him, blood running out of his mouth.
RICK	Mike!
	MIKE wakes up again, screaming. This time he is truly alone.

Scene Eight

Simultaneously, RICK's apartment/MIKE's room from previous scene. RICK wakes up screaming. MIKE puts away his texts and reaches for his notebook by the side of the bed. RICK reaches for the remote for his video camera. They both begin recording.

MIKE	Ching-Shih, period. Female vampire period. Something of a legend comma with a little bit of truth mixed in period.
RICK	Baseline Video number 18. Trouble sleeping again. Must be the drugs losing effect. Remember to up the prescription.
MIKE	She is all hunger comma no empathy comma no soul period. The mythology comma ancestry comma I don't know where it comes from.
RICK	Had a dream about.... Dark hair. Black eyes, darker than sin itself. Blood-stained teeth, sharpened canines with shreds of flesh hanging off them.
RICK/MIKE	Ching-Shih—
MIKE	—period. Exists in the stories from our youth comma in our cultural consciousness comma in our blood period.
RICK	I woke up calling Mike's name. Not sure why. Tasmin's away, or she would have had questions. I am beginning to hate her.
MIKE	The vampire is not important comma the embodiment comma the manifestation period. She is not the heart period.
RICK	I couldn't stop thinking about her. This creature. This monstrosity. She was familiar, like a scar you forgot you had. *(pause)* She loved me.
MIKE	He is not afraid of her comma not afraid comma not afraid not afraid not afraid ellipsis.
RICK/MIKE	Ching-Shih—
RICK	She's coming to get me. My history.

> *Beat.*

Baseline Video 18. Over and out.

MIKE	Period.

ACT TWO: THE QUEST™: *In which they search tirelessly*

Scene One

SHEL is on his cell phone. He is calling Kathy.

SHEL   C'mon, pick up pick up pick up…

He gets her machine.

Hi Kath. It's Shel. *(pause)* Again. I can't seem to get a hold of you. I was wondering if… uh, if you knew for sure which dates I can come back up to see you. I was hoping I could come up early on the seventh. Let me know. Okay. So… call me. Love you lots, baby. Bye.

He hangs up. He is unsettled.

Scene Two

All five boys are at the Bomb Shelter, a popular Waterloo pub. It is their third year. Mina, MIKE's long time girlfriend, has just left him. He is staring, dismally, into his beer. The other boys gather around him.

MIKE   Why do women always want to "talk about it"?

DAVE   Nature of the beast.

SHEL   And what a beast…

MIKE   She stops me, in the middle of the quad, between classes to break up with me.

LUKE   The sweetest revenge, Mike, is healing. That's my best advice.

DAVE   My best advice is that you need another drink.

SHEL   Maybe she just needs time.

MIKE   She's had time.

SHEL   If you give her the space she needs…

MIKE	She's had space.
SHEL	Mike, if you love something… I mean if you *really* love something.
MIKE	So help me God, Shel, if you say "let it go, and it will come back to you" I will kill your family in their sleep.

Awkward silence.

DAVE	That's the spirit! More tequila!

They down more tequila.

I swear, if I ever catch my ex with another dude, I'll fuckin' Ninja his ass.

LUKE	"Ninja" is not a verb, Dave.
DAVE	A Ninja is whatever the fuck it wants to be. That's why they wear masks.
SHEL	But isn't it better, guys, to have loved and lost, than never to have—
ALL	Shut up, Shel.
LUKE	A really important Zen guy said that love is an illusion. Life is suffering, and—
DAVE	They're all bitches, Mike, you're better off without—

RICK now interrupts by striking a match off the table and lighting his cigarette. He smokes. They listen, captivated.

RICK	Sexloverelationships. One word. They're the same fucking thing, just a semantic argument apart. You keep them together; you control it, the power is in your hands. You separate them; and you're inviting pain and anguish into your home. The moment sexloverelationships becomes a "relationship" is the moment you give it enough power to destroy you. Same with "love." Even "sex," once you define it apart from the others, it becomes a holy grail. Desperation follows. The Quest. It's all in vain.
	Sexloverelationships is everywhere. It's ripe for the picking. It's not something you search for.

(He sees the boys are confused.) Okay, look. Who's the one girl you've all lusted after but know you'll never get close to?

ALL	Daphne.

RICK	Right. Daphne the-fuck-machine Chan. Here's Daphne's dilemma: She'd really like to fuck you reverse-cowgirl with her black leather thigh-high boots on. Honestly. But she can't. You know why? Here's what Daphne sees: She looks at Shel, she sees a guy looking for "love." Dave, he's just looking for "sex." Luke, couldn't possibly have a relationship to save his life. And Mikey...

But when Daphne looks at me she sees every possibility open to her. Sexloverelationships – the whole package.

MIKE	You're saying you had sex with Daphne?

RICK	No. I'm saying I had a deep, meaningful relationship with Daphne – over the course of which I fucked her cock-eyed. It had all the satisfaction of a long term relationship, with none of the heartbreak.

> *Simultaneously:*

SHEL	Go, Rick!

LUKE	Nicely done!

DAVE	Cock-eyed! Nice!

MIKE	Rick. Congratulations and everything, but... it's not the same. It's nothing like love. Love is... love is those perfect little moments. Like... like when Mina and I would go out for sushi, and there's always an odd number of salmon sashimi, y'notice that? And we'd always get down to the last one, and she'd flick her chopsticks and tell me I could have it. But I'd say "no, no, you go ahead." Even if I was starving. Even if it was the best sashimi I'd ever tasted... I let her have the last piece. Because I knew she wanted it. And the way she smiled when she got it. Like she'd just won a prize. It was perfect.

> *Pause. The boys look at MIKE, quizzically. Then back to RICK.*

SHEL	Daphne Chan?
LUKE	You really had sex with her?
DAVE	Did you keep the condom?

> *MIKE is miffed.*

MIKE   Forget it, you guys don't understand. You're not... you're not even paying attention. *(beat)* Daphne Chan. Good work, Rick. Way to go. *(He gets up to leave.)* I gotta go to class.

> *He begins walking out of the bar. The other boys are still questioning RICK, who rises and catches up with MIKE at the door.*

RICK   Mike! *(MIKE turns.)* I didn't mean to... I mean, I wasn't saying that to...

MIKE   I know. S'okay.

RICK   You're better off without her. I really mean that.

MIKE   Sure. I'll see you.

> *He starts off.*

RICK   Mike...

MIKE   Yah.

RICK   *(tentatively, almost paranoid)* The last piece? Really?

MIKE   Every time.

> *Pause.*

RICK   What's that feel like? To do that?

> *Pause. MIKE ponders.*

MIKE   It's nice. It's like... the opposite of guilt.

> *Pause.*

RICK   Hm. I'll see you 'round Chao.

MIKE   Yah. See you.

> *MIKE leaves. RICK goes back to The Boys.*

Scene Three

SHEL is on his cell phone. He is calling Kathy.

SHEL   C'mon, pick up pick up pick up…

Machine again.

Hey baby. I was just wondering if you wanted… uh… if
you wanted me to bring your… your hair elastic, when
I see you. You left it here, and… uh… if you want it, I can
bring it, I know how you like… ponytails. Okay. I'll just
pack it.

He starts to hang up.

But… maybe I shouldn't in case you got a new one. That
way you can have one here and one there. That would
be… I mean, for convenience. Okay, I'll just… I'll bring
it.

He starts to hang up.

Sorry, just… the last time I talked to you, you said you
were thinking of getting a haircut, so if you were getting
a haircut, then I should just leave it here. The hair elastic.
Just, because short hair is… more manageable. I guess.
I'll leave it.

He starts to hang up.

Or I could…

Pause. He hits a button on the phone.

MACHINE   Message erased.

He hangs up. He is unsettled.

Scene Four

*MIKE is in his room, studying for the MCATs. He is
struggling. Mental White Noise begins to fill the room.
It debilitates him. He is unable to think. His ears begin
to bleed. Desperately, he pulls out the Campbell's soup*

box from under his bed. He withdraws a notebook. He begins writing, breathlessly, as if he is drowning.

MIKE There once was a man full of words. Period. They spilled out when he yawned, shot out when he coughed, slid from his pores, off tendril fingers on to the floor. Wasted. Prisoners, they inhabited him. He was their Angel Island, a halfway house between here and there, comma, then and now... but he could never escape them. They were always with him, overflowing from him... dripping from his brow into his cup of coffee. Period, end of paragraph.

The Mental White Noise lessens. He writes.

One day the man was poised over paper, and watched the words spill from his fingertips on to the page. Transfixed, entranced, curious – he spilled more, then poured them out, as many as he could... but he was never drained. The pages filled, he wept volumes, sweat omnibus editions... he ran out of surface before he ran out of words. He had found a way to set them free.

The Mental White Noise is almost gone.

He was free. And he would never lose his way again. He knew what he had to do. Period.

The Mental White Noise is gone. He is saved. Then, he shamefully writes a new sentence.

So he became a doctor to please his mother.

Scene Five

SHEL is pacing up and down his room, cell phone in hand. It rings.

SHEL Kathy?

Pause. He listens.

No, thank you, I already subscribe to the *Star*.

He paces. He makes a call.

Hi, Cynthia, it's Shel. Kathy's boyfriend. Yah, look I'm trying to get a hold of— *(pause)* Uh huh. *(pause)* Busy. Exams, right. That time of year. Okay if you— *(pause)* No, don't tell her that I… just ask her to call me. Please. Thank you.

> *He hangs up. Paces. He makes another call.*

Hey, Happy Chan, what's going on, it's Shel. Hey, you remember that guy Kathy dated before me? What was his name: Rui? You don't have his number, do you? *(He writes it down.)* Thanks, Happy.

> *He hangs up. Still unsettled.*

Scene Six

> *DAVE is at JEANETTE's house. She is in the washroom, freshening up. He is holding an empty condom wrapper that is clearly not his.*

DAVE   Was it like you remembered?

JEANETTE   *(off)* I'm sorry?

DAVE   When you fucked your ex-boyfriend today. Was it like you remembered?

> *Pause. JEANETTE comes out of the bathroom. DAVE waves the empty wrapper.*

Not my brand, sweetheart.

JEANETTE   When did you know?

DAVE   I stopped by earlier. His Harley was parked out front. Same old bike, dents and scratches all over it.

JEANETTE   His bike doesn't have a scratch on it.

DAVE   Does now.

JEANETTE   You… oh, God, David you are such a child.

DAVE   And being a lying, cheating bitch is the hallmark of maturity?

JEANETTE	Fuck you.
DAVE	Obviously, you're the grown-up.
JEANETTE	I just can't deal with you anymore.
DAVE	The fuck does that mean?
JEANETTE	It means… it means what it means.
DAVE	Christ, you sound like Luke.
JEANETTE	God, you're not gonna lay more of this "Banana Boy" shit on me, are you?
DAVE	Excuse me?
JEANETTE	Whenever something doesn't go your way, or there's any kind of problem, it's all because of something intangible you have no control over: like being Chinese. And instead of solving your problems, you wind up drinking yourself into an oblivion and pass out, only to wake up back where you started, only more bitter and more cynical and angrier and… and… and… *(She gives up and starts back into the bathroom.)*
DAVE	No, no, keep going, I'm on the edge of my seat. What else is wrong with me, Jeanette?
JEANETTE	What *isn't* wrong with you? Look at you: You're broke. You have no ambition. And when you're not fiddling with your fucking computer, you're at the bar with your loser friends drinking your faces off.
DAVE	Okay, first of all, I don't "fiddle," I'm a fucking computer *engineer.* Second, don't you *dare* bring The Boys into this, they've done nothing to you. Third… I'll get back to you on the ambition thing… because I can't think of something real snappy right now.
JEANETTE	You just… you don't get any better than this, do you?
DAVE	I didn't know I was supposed to.
JEANETTE	Yeah, Dave. *(beat)* We're all supposed to.

> Pause. DAVE speaks in an aside, almost to himself, while JEANETTE rants at him. At points they overlap, but their speeches are not totally simultaneous.

DAVE	This isn't really happening. This isn't... I can't...
JEANETTE	David, you've been terrified of life from the day I met you.
DAVE	I've been so good to you, so fucking good...
JEANETTE	You can't even take care of yourself.
DAVE	This was supposed to be the one good thing, the one true thing...
JEANETTE	Accept it, Dave. This isn't a fight you can win.
DAVE	It's not fair! To be in love, for *me* to be in love, and now this?
JEANETTE	You can't make this go away with snide remarks and rhetoric.
DAVE	No, I don't believe this. It's not happening.
JEANETTE	It's real. It's happening.

Pause.

It's already happened.

Beat.

DAVE Who's gonna love me, Jeanette? Who can love this, if not you? You saw something in me. Something worth loving, I don't know what. And if you.... Who's gonna find that thing again? So, maybe... maybe you could tell me what it is. And... and I won't ask you for anything else, I won't even ask for my stuff back... maybe just tell me that thing you saw in me. And then I'll... I'll just go.

Pause.

JEANETTE You were happy once, Dave. I remember you were... what happened?

Pause.

DAVE *(in denial)* Nothing! Okay, nothing happened, I... *(He gives up, and is painfully sincere.)* I don't know.

JEANETTE   I'm going to go out for an hour. Take what you want,
            I can mail the rest, or... you should probably not be here
            when I get back.

            *JEANETTE goes to DAVE, they stand awkwardly, not
            touching. She tries to touch him, but he recoils. She
            leaves. DAVE is motionless. He stares, blank.*

DAVE   And so it begins...

Scene Seven

*SHEL stares at his cell phone. He starts to dial several
times, and abandons it. Finally, reluctantly, he dials.*

SHEL   Hello, is this Rui Wan? Hi, my name is... Shel... man...
            Kwan... g. "Shelman Kwang" yes. I'm calling from the
            Ottawa Citizen, we're having a subscription special and—
            (pause) Well someone had contacted us from this
            address, does a Kathy Yim live there? *(relieved)* She
            doesn't! Er... she doesn't? *(pause)* But she... does... stay
            there quite often. I see. *(pause)* Well, she's rather fond of
            the... the *Citizen,* I guess. And... I'll try and reach her
            another time. Thank you. *(pause)* Um, sorry, just...
            (pause) She likes it when you warm up her side of the
            bed before she goes to sleep. Just lie there for a minute or
            two before she gets in, so it's not too cold for her. She,
            uh... she likes that.

            He hangs up. Still unsettled.

Scene Eight

*The Boys are gathered in the Bomb Shelter around
DAVE's laptop. They are constructing the Perfect Girl.
Cut images of different girls; the head of one, the
breasts of another, the ass of another, are scattered
projections around them. DAVE is using PhotoShop,
and the projections move to overlap and form the*

> *Perfect Girl around them. Luke stands by, not participating.*

DAVE   Okay, now the breasts.

MIKE   Shannon Elizabeth!

SHEL   Nice.

> *Shannon Elizabeth's breasts slide down under Hsu Chi's face.*

RICK   What about Salma Hayek?

DAVE   I like the ethnic angle.

> *The breasts change to Salma Hayek's.*

Next!

SHEL   Booty.

ALL   J-Lo!

> *J-Lo's ass slides in.*

MIKE   Have we considered Kylie Minogue?

> *Kylie's ass slides in.*

All in favour?

MIKE/DAVE Aye.

MIKE   All opposed?

SHEL/RICK Aye.

MIKE   We've got a stalemate. Luke?

LUKE   Whatever.

DAVE   I'm counting that as a vote for Kylie.

RICK   Don't fuck with J-Lo.

DAVE   So use your computer. Next!

MIKE   Legs.

SHEL   Famke Janssen. From "X-Men," Jean Grey!

DAVE   Love Jean Grey.

Famke's legs slide in.

Almost done… just give her some metal bracelets, à la Linda Carter…

ALL   Wonder Woman!

DAVE   And we're done.

The image is a disjointed jigsaw puzzle of body parts, with the file name: "Perfect_Girl.jpg."

ALL   Beautiful.

LUKE stares blankly at her.

LUKE   S'okay…

DAVE   And you can do better?

LUKE   I think so…

LUKE takes the helm of the computer. He fiddles around, and deletes all the images. He saves the blank file as "Reality.jpg." Pause.

RICK   Leave it to the psych major.

DAVE   I don't get it.

LUKE   And the harder you look, the more disappointed you're gonna be.

He walks off. The Boys look at each other expectantly.

DAVE   I get it. *(beat)* Luke's gay.

Scene Nine

War. The battlefield of Love. Machine guns fire. Bombs drop. Hearts break. The Boys are armed in John Woo style. SHEL wheels MIKE off in a gurney, a sheet over him. An arrow marked "Unrealistic Career" sticks out of the sheet.

SHEL   It's Private Chao. He's down.

DAVE   Goddammit! We've got no Privates left!

LUKE	Incoming!
	Gunfire.
DAVE	Dammit, they're everywhere! It's a goddamn epidemic!
SHEL	They're in the trees! They're in the trees!!!
LUKE	Rice King, 3 o'clock!
	DAVE kills him.
SHEL	Watch your six!
	DAVE whips around and kills another.
LUKE	9 o'clock, Abercrombie!
	SHEL kills him.
DAVE	Any sign of Fitch?
SHEL	Not yet. But we'll get him.
LUKE	Sarge, they've got us outnumbered!
DAVE	Keep fighting, soldiers!
	SHEL fires off a few rounds, but he gets hit in the knee.
SHEL	I've been hit! Sarge! I've been hit!
LUKE	There's too many of 'em, retreat!
DAVE	No! This is war, goddammit! And it's gonna get ugly! Take a look.
	They huddle as DAVE draws a map-like document.
SHEL	What is that, Sarge?
DAVE	It's a Venn diagram! Now pay attention jarhead and you'll see how badly the battle is being lost in the jungles of love and relationships. See here – this circle represents White girls. They quite naturally intersect with White guys.
LUKE	And Asian guys? White girls don't intersect with Asian guys?
DAVE	Nope, soldier. To them we're too geeky, and quite possibly all gay. Now you'll see that the White guys'll intersect

with anything. They're at the top of the sociological ladder. Notice how a large portion of them intersect with Asian women. As do a sub-section of Black guys.

SHEL   What's that over there?

DAVE   That's the East Indians – who for the most part find love running through fields, singing and dancing like they do on Channel 47.

LUKE   Sarge! In the trees!

DAVE fires a few rounds off into the trees.

DAVE   Thanks, soldier. Now over here, we've got The Orientals. These circles represent FOBs – mostly HK FOBs but you can stack in Taiwanese and Koreans in there too. They are an island to themselves. The chicks want a guy with a nice car and lots of money and the guys want someone who'll match the upholstery of their souped-up Integra.

LUKE   It's all so complex! How we ever gonna break through!

DAVE   If you think *those* were hard, this here's the mother of all impenetrable fortresses – the Banana Girls. If they don't study a bajillion hours a day, they'll go for White guys, Black guys, Jewish guys, Indian guys, purple guys all guys except for… you guessed it…. The Banana Boys of the world. We got… well, uh… we got exotic fish, Quake, Internet porn…

SHEL   But *why*, Sarge? It's so unfair!

LUKE   Are we not good looking enough? Is that it?

DAVE   Absolutely not, soldier! In fact, I think the both of you have very pretty eyes.

They stare at each other awkwardly.

Anyway. There is one group I didn't mention. Black Ops. Deep cover.

He draws a circle that encompasses every other circle.

They fit in everywhere. They're just so damn attractive that no one, not even the enemy, is impervious to their charms.

> *RICK walks on. Bullets bounce off him. He saunters across the stage, half-naked.*

Look at him. Bullet-proof. Unharmed by stereotypes and desired by all.

> *RICK waves to the guys. They salute half-heartedly.*

RICK   Hoo-ah!!

ALL 3   *(unenthusiastic)* Hoo-ah.

> *He saunters off.*

DAVE   War really is Hell.

> *Suddenly an air raid siren is heard.*

SHEL   What is that!

> *There's a sudden whistling that cuts through the air and an explosion as a bomb clearly labelled "Small Penis" pins DAVE.*

SARGE!!!

LUKE   Banana down! Banana down!

DAVE   I'm hit guys! And I'm not getting up from this one! Go – go on without me! Knock those ign'ant motherfuckers clear outta the water! Give 'em hell! Give 'em hell!!!!

> *The sound of gunfire and explosions rise, as DAVE · dies. LUKE and SHEL go off, guns blazing.*

Scene Ten

> *SHEL is still on his cell phone call, leaving a message for Kathy.*

SHEL   Kathy. *(pause)* I'm coming to Ottawa. Meet me at the Tim Hortons by your house at 2 o'clock. *(pause)* I think we should talk.

> *He hangs up. Still unsettled.*

Scene One

LUKE is applying for a loan at the bank.

LUKE	So, yah, I was thinking about two grand should do it.
BANKER	Do you have an account with Canada Trust?
LUKE	No.
BANKER	Where do you normally do your banking?
LUKE	Sock & Associates Trust Fund.
BANKER	I'm not familiar with them. Where are they located?
LUKE	Top drawer of my dresser. *(blank stare)* Get it? Sock & Associates? *(blank stare)* I have a sock. I keep my money in it.
BANKER	I see. And the associates?
LUKE	The rest of my socks. *(pause)* And underwear.
BANKER	Is this a joke, Mr. Yeung?
LUKE	No, no, I swear. I'm being very serious.
BANKER	Hm. You are employed, aren't you?

> *Shift. LUKE is at an interview with the Edge 102. ALAN Cross is offering him a job.*

ALAN	Would you like to be here, Luke?
LUKE	At the Edge 102? I don't know. S'a good station.
ALAN	I was a big fan of your program on CMSH. The "Morning Mosh" with "The Yeungster." I liked it. I liked it a lot. And I'd like to offer you an opportunity here at the Edge.
LUKE	Oh yeah?
ALAN	What do you think?
LUKE	I don't know…
ALAN	A three-year contract.

l to r: David Yee, Dale Yim, Derek Kwan, Richard Lee, Insurp Choi
photo by Guy Bertrand

LUKE	*(This is three years longer than the longest commitment LUKE has ever made.)* Three years…
ALAN	Luke, I'm offering you security. A real job. The chance to make a living, doing what you love. What more could you want?
	Shift. LUKE is at the Bomb Shelter with MIKE and RICK.
MIKE	You're dropping out? For real?
RICK	Good for you!
LUKE	What is this place teaching me, anyway?
MIKE	You gotta finish.
LUKE	Why? Why are we so bent on "finishing" things? I mean, maybe I am finished, right? Maybe this is me, being finished.

MIKE   Psychology isn't like business or engineering, where you can complete your education in the workplace. No one's gonna want a psychologist that gave up halfway through. What if they have abandonment issues? That's not very reassuring.

RICK   Let's put this in perspective: Luke, how much do you make in one night, DJ-ing?

LUKE   Couple hundred?

RICK   And you're good at it?

LUKE   *(quietly, self-consciously)* Yah... I think I am.

RICK   Well there you go. Kid makes a couple hundred bucks a night doing what he's fuckin' good at. What he's got a talent for. *(pointed)* You could learn something from him, Mikey.

MIKE   But there's no job security!

    Shift. Banker.

BANKER   Perhaps someone could co-sign for you. Your mother?

LUKE   Naw, she wouldn't...

BANKER   Your father, then?

LUKE   I... uh, don't have one.

BANKER   You don't...?

LUKE   He took off.

BANKER   Oh. Well, Oliver Twist, I guess no one loves you.

LUKE   That's... so... mean.

    Shift. The Edge 102.

ALAN   Whadd'ya say bucko?

LUKE   I don't know... so what if you give me this, right? And then it doesn't work out? Say, I refuse to play Nickelback, or Default, or Theory of a Deadman, 'cause (let's face it) it's all the same band. What if I do that? And then we're both stuck with a raw deal: You thought you were getting a guy that'd play Theory of a Nickel-fault, and I thought I was going somewhere I could express myself.

ALAN   I love Nickelback.

Shift. Bomb Shelter.

LUKE   DJ-ing is what I love doing.

MIKE   Like you loved psychology?

LUKE   I changed my mind.

MIKE   What if you change it again?

LUKE   Then that's what I was meant to do. The universe is trying to tell me something.

MIKE   That you're indecisive?

Shift. LUKE is at the store, buying a chocolate bar.

LUKE   Snickers, please.

He buys the Snickers, then reconsiders.

Actually, could I get a Kit Kat? Thanks. Sorry.

He buys it, and reconsiders again.

Sorry, just… it's not a "wafer" kind of day, could I get a Three Musketeers?

He buys it, reconsiders.

Okay, so I thought it wasn't a wafer day, but maybe just not a crispy wafer, and I actually want a creamy wafer. Could I get a Choclair?

Pause.

Ah, fuck it. *(He leaves.)*

Shift. The Edge 102.

ALAN   I'm gonna have to ask you to leave my office now.

Shift. Bomb Shelter.

RICK   Mike and I got a student thing to do. See you around.

Shift. Bank.

LUKE	Look, I need this loan. I've got no employable skills, no credit, no savings and I'm running out of options like peanuts at a ballgame. So if you don't help me, Mr. Banker-Man, then you may as well be putting the final nail in my coffin. I hope you can live with the guilt.
BANKER	*(pause)* I'm pretty sure I can.
LUKE	I'm going to leave now.
BANKER	I think that would be best.
	LUKE leaves, but as he leaves he screams to the bank customers.
LUKE	Canada Trust can go to Hell!

Scene Two

MIKE is part of the Banana Banana Number One Pageant. A Game Show from Hell. The Announcer speaks.

ANN.	Laaadies and gentlemen, welcome welcome to the Banana Banana Number One! Pageant. Where every man's a king and every king's a momma's boy!
	Our first contestant, Michael Chao is vying for the role of Number One Son! Are you ready Michael?
MIKE	What am I doing here?
MOM	Go Mikoh! Go Number One Boy!
ANN.	For this stage we have a sealed envelope, guaranteed by the firm of Jones and Lavoie containing a skill-testing question, which you must answer to move on. Are you ready?
MIKE	Ready? Who said I even wanna play?
MOM	Go Mi-Koh! Go! Go!
MIKE	Mom?

ANN.	May I have the envelope please. Michael.... What do you want to be when you grow up? A) A Doctor, B) A Lawyer, C) A Businessman or D) An Engineer?
MIKE	Umm well really… umm, hmmm, I've always wanted to be a writer.
ANN.	Heh-heh, I don't think you heard me right son the ONLY choices were A) Doctor, B) Lawyer, C) Businessman, or D) Engineer.
MOM	Doctor! Mi-Koh! Say Doctor! A! A! Tell him letter A!
MIKE	No, honestly… I'd really like to try to become a writer.
ANN.	Whoo, umm well, I'm sorry – that answer disqualifies you!
MOM	Nooo! Why you want say you want write *siu gou jei* – small baby tales! Why Mi-koh? Why you do this to your mama? *(wailing)* Oh your dad and I, we had such big hopes for you! Where did we go wrong? Where did we go wrong? This not good, Mikoh. Not good. We not let you ruin life like this!
ANN.	Oooh! Does that sound like a challenge? According to pageant rules, when a challenge is put forth then we automatically move to the Panda Power Round!
MIKE	What the hell's a Panda Power Round?
MOM	After all we give you, after piano lessons, math camp, Commodore 64, you want to throw it all away! Well that's not going to happen!
	As she is speaking MOM enters wearing an inflatable rubber sumo suit.
MIKE	Mom! What the fuck!?!
MOM	Watch your mouth Mikoh!
ANN.	So Michael, in the Panda Power round, we repeat the question. A) Doctor, B) Lawyer—
MIKE	I told you none of the ab—
	MOM runs at him and butts him with her sumo belly. He drops to his knees in pain.

MOM   What will Auntie Amy say!?!

MIKE   But Mom!

              She puts him in a full nelson.

MOM   How you make money as a writer?

MIKE   Can't I even have a chance to prove—

              She flips him on his back.

MOM   Who'll take care of us when we're old?

MIKE   Don't you believe in m—

              She gives him a belly splash.

MOM   Don't you love your mama?

MIKE   But!

              She splashes him again. MIKE is clearly in pain.

MOM   Why do you want to break your mama's heart!

MIKE   I don't!

MOM   Do you hate your parents, Mikoh?

              With every line she splashes MIKE and his suffering increases with each drop until he is completely spent.

MIKE   Please stop!

MOM   We love you Mikoh!

MIKE   Please! No!

MOM   We love you!!!

MIKE   Please! Please stop! Stop! Stop! No! No more! Enough!

ANN.   A. Doctor B. Lawyer, C. Businessman, or D. Engineer.

MIKE   Letter A damn you. Letter A, Doctor. I will be a doctor.

              MOM, who at this point is sitting atop him, gives him a gentle kiss on the forehead.

MOM   We love you Mikoh. You thank us later.

Scene Three

RICK gets to his dorm room. He is a little buzzed and staggers on to his bed. A light in the corner flips on. MIKE is sitting on the opposite side of the room. He throws RICK's pills at him. RICK catches them without flinching.

MIKE   Pyloxidin?

RICK   Was looking for these.

He pops a few. Beat.

MIKE   Rick, that shit's bad for you.

RICK   Is that your expert medical opinion, Dr. Chao?

MIKE   It is.

RICK   I'll take it under advisement.

He pops another pill, downing it with alcohol.

MIKE   You shouldn't take that with alcohol. It's an anti-depressant.

RICK   It's a performance enhancer.

MIKE   I didn't think you needed any "enhancing," Rick.

RICK   Better living through chemistry, that's what I always say.

MIKE   I've never heard you say that.

RICK   I just started.

Beat.

How's the book coming along?

MIKE   What does that have to do with anything?

RICK   Don't be defensive.

MIKE   *(defensively)* I'm not being defensive.

Beat.

RICK   You have the potential to be a great writer, Mike.

MIKE   I'm trying to work, Rick. Stop distracting me.

RICK	You lack focus.
MIKE	I don't—
RICK	The drug will give you that focus. The drive. The necessary tools to succeed. It'll bring out your talent, and the book—whatever it's about—will get written, and we'll all be famous.
MIKE	Don't do that.
RICK	Do what?
MIKE	Turn on your salesman routine.
RICK	*(a sales pitch)* Pyloxidin. The Wonder Drug. Eliminates depression, while enhancing key traits deemed beneficial in the world economy – confidence, independence, self-esteem—
MIKE	You're not paying attention! Do you know what this does to your brain chemistry?
RICK	Turns down the suck and turns up the happy?
MIKE	It's like Ecstasy, but stronger. It's like Ecstasy on Heroin.
RICK	Don't mix your metaphors.
MIKE	Don't tell me what to do with my metaphors.
RICK	Don't tell me—
MIKE	It boosts your serotonin levels so high that you could have a serotongenetic response. From there, it's anyone's guess: aneurysm, dementia, cognitive failure… death…
RICK	…power, success, money, women. Means to an end. Sure, the end sucks. But you gotta admit the means are pretty damn enticing.
	Beat.
MIKE	I'm worried about you.
RICK	And I'm worried about you. Your life, your misery, this angst… it could all be over.
MIKE	Forget it, I can't just have a… I'm going to sleep. Good night. *(He turns off the light.)*

Beat.

RICK   Mike?

MIKE   What?

RICK   Are you mad?

MIKE   No.

RICK   You are. Don't go to bed angry. C'mon.

MIKE   I'm not mad. Good night.

Beat.

RICK   I'm sorry.

MIKE   You always say that.

RICK   I really am sorry. I promise.

Beat. RICK turns the lights back on.

What's the thing you hate most in the world, Mike?

Pause. Hesitation.

MIKE   I… I don't know… let's just go to sleep.

He turns off the lights. RICK turns them back on.

RICK   C'mon… you gotta hate *something*.

MIKE   I hate being interrogated. Good night.

He turns off the lights.

RICK   *(hurt)* Fine.

MIKE turns on the lights.

MIKE   Are you mad?

RICK   No. It was just a question, but if you don't *trust me* then fine. Good night.

MIKE   It's not—

RICK   Good night.

RICK turns off the lights. Pause.

MIKE   I hate… Mental White Noise.

> *RICK turns on the lights.*

RICK　　And the cure to Mental White Noise… *(He offers him the bottle of pills.)* …is right here. Focus, in a 40mg pill. That's like, that's like… hope in a mason jar.

MIKE　　Nothing's that easy, Rick.

RICK　　Try it. Try it once, and you'll see how focused you become. You can shut out the Mental White Noise. Your dreams will be within reach. *(He puts them in MIKE's hand.)* Choose, Mike. The Noise, or *The Book.* It's a remarkably simple decision.

> *Beat.*
>
> *RICK slowly becomes less lucid, mindshifting into the future. MIKE stares at the pills, almost longingly.*

MIKE　　Nothing's that easy. Is it?

RICK　　Only one way to find out, Mikey. *(shift)* Baseline. *(shift)* You have control now over— *(shift)* Baseline. *(shift)* —over how the story turns out. *(Shift)* Baseline Video number 17.

MIKE　　What?

RICK　　Remember to pick up Tasmin from the airport on Sunday. *(shift)* What's it going to be, Mike?

MIKE　　Who's Tasmin?

RICK　　I don't know. Is she hot? *(shift)* Meeting with six-figure client on Monday afternoon. Golf again, then karaoke. *(shift)* Mike?

MIKE　　What's happening?

RICK　　I'm mindshifting, Mike. Keep track of me. Like I told you, I'll need my— *(shift)* Get your bearings looked at, the Beamer's rattling a bit. Could be trouble later— *(shift)* Gotta go, Mikey. I'll be back soon.

> *RICK passes out on the bed. MIKE watches him for a bit, still considering the pills. He hesitates, then sits down and takes up a piece of paper and a pen. He writes a message for RICK.*

Name: *Richard Wong. Age: 23.*

Status: *3rd year BComm, U of Waterloo.*

Notes: *Get bearings looked at. Could be trouble later.*

> *MIKE places the paper beside RICK's head. Discreetly, he takes RICK's pulse. It's reasonable. He considers the pills. Almost against his own will, he puts them in his pocket, and walks out of the room.*

Scene Four

> *SHEL at dragon boat practice. BROCK Landers and CHEST Rockwell are the team captains.*

COACH	Alright, Captains, pick your teams for dragon boat racing.
BROCK	Chip Whitmore.
CHEST	Rocco.
BROCK	The Vanderbilt twins.
CHEST	Whitley Whiterson.
BROCK	Richie Moneybags the 3rd.
CHEST	Richie Moneybags the 4th.
BROCK	Aloysius Cunningham.
CHEST	Pippy Longstocking.
BROCK	Lady Diana.
CHEST	Daddy Warbucks.
BROCK	The cast of "90210."
CHEST	The Canadian Broadcasting Corporation.
BROCK	Damn, that DaVinci can row. Um… the pool boy.
CHEST	The… the gardener.
BROCK	The adopted Somalian children.

CHEST	The autistic guy.
BROCK	*(realizing no one's left, but SHEL)* Heavens, Chest, who's left?
CHEST	Well, Brock… looks like… just Sheldon Kwan.
BROCK	I'll trade you Tori Spelling—
CHEST	Not a chance.
BROCK	Fine… Sheldon… I guess.

Scene Five

DAVE is standing next to a White guy. Unprovoked, he punches the White guy in the face.

DAVE   **Racial Incident Log. Incident:** #581.

Date: June 5th.

Notes: Generic Abercrombie White boy standing on a street corner, not really doing anything. But he looked at me. Looked at me like he was gonna do something. Something… White. And… racist. So I punched him in the mouth and took his wallet.

Grade: D-.

Comments: I think I may need help. *(pause)* Ah, who am I kidding? Good job, soldier! For that, you get a Coke!

Scene Six

The Boys walk, one by one, on stage. They sit with their backs to the audience. Like mannequins. Slowly, they begin to pose. They come together to raise glasses. A picture is taken. The picture is of The Boys laughing and drinking at the Bomb Shelter. RICK is in the centre. They look young, drunk, and happy. RICK is the happiest of them all. It's his family portrait.

Scene Seven

RICK is in his condo, getting ready to go to work. He slips a Berlitz Tape: "FOB Today!" into a tape player, and begins his morning workout regiment.

TAPE   Thank you for choosing the Berlitz Language School to learn how to speak FOB. *(beat)* "Fawb. Fresh-Off-The-Boat. Noun. A derogatory slang phrase applied to people of foreign nationality...

RICK fast forwards the tape to the end of the definition.

...the T is silent. Like in "borsht." *(beat)* This tape will not only teach you the basics of the FOB language, but how to interact within the FOB culture seamlessly. So get ready to cast aside your *Jook Sing* identity! *(beat)* "Joke Sing." Noun. Translated as Hollow Bamboo, used to define Canadian-born-Chinese. See "Banana..."

RICK fast forwards again.

You're just another Hong Konger, fresh off the boat, looking for a pack of Marlboros and some Hello Kitty! paraphernalia for your Integra.

RICK   *(holds up a small, stuffed Hello Kitty! doll)* Check. *(He lights up a Marlboro... with a Hello Kitty! lighter.)* Check.

TAPE   FOBs are an integral part of today's world economy. Bananas become data entry clerks, minimum wage slaves. FOBs become CEOs, high-ranking corporate executives, and all around winners in the game of Life.

RICK   I am a winner... *(He clears his throat, and adjusts his accent.)* ...a winner in the game of Life.

TAPE   To have a strong identity is to have a strong presence in the market, in business and in life. What's your identity?

RICK   *(in perfect FOB)* I'm one of you.

Beat.

TAPE   You're doing great. Please turn to side B.

RICK   Please turn to side B. *(He laughs, and pops a few pills, chasing them with alcohol.)* You're doing great. *(He adjusts.)* You're doing…. You're doing great.

> *He flips to Side B, and begins to dress. He throws on a shirt and tie, then sits in front of the mirror. He begins to slowly, carefully, almost sexually, apply makeup to his face.*

TAPE   Welcome to Side B, Rick.

> *Rick looks at the tape player. He shrugs. When the TAPE plays again, it is RICK's voice coming out of it.*

You need to be lighter.

> *RICK applies foundation, lightening his skin tone.*

Poor people are dark. Low class mainland bottom feeders. You are no longer from Scarborough. You are from Causeway Bay. You spent afternoons shopping in Tsim Sha Tsui, and torturing the boat people on the Harbour, because they were darker than you. Class is everything. And everything is class.

> *RICK examines himself.*

Perfect. *(pause)* Did you remember to moisturize?

> *RICK nods.*

Good boy. Next are the eyes.

> *RICK uses eyeliner to outline his eyes.*

The shape of perfect almonds. Smooth, curvature is sexy, almost female. Give shadow. Not bags. Mystery. Allure. Seduction. Become the inscrutable Chinese. The insatiable Chinese.

> *RICK has finished his eyes. They are exotic, and female.*

Lips.

> *RICK applies lipstick to his mouth.*

Red. Wet. Pulsing. A heartbeat.

> *RICK looks himself over in the mirror. He is grotesque.*
> *He looks as if he is embalmed.*

Look at you. You're beautiful. A perfect FOB.

> *RICK smiles.*

Leave the Banana Boys. Get rid of them. You don't need them anymore.

RICK What?

> *He rewinds the tape.*

TAPE They're useless to you. *Jook Sing*, only hold you back.

RICK No.

TAPE Empty baggage. Dull-witted.

RICK Stop it.

TAPE Shameful.

RICK You don't know them.

TAPE Tedious.

RICK Friends, they're my—

TAPE Sycophants. You're better than them.

RICK I... am I?

TAPE Successful. Assured. Charming.

RICK I am.

TAPE Powerful. Desirable.

RICK Yes.

TAPE Be one of us.

RICK I... will.

TAPE She'll love you.

> *RICK is dreamy.*

RICK Who will love me?

TAPE The Ching-Shih.

RICK snaps around.

RICK What?

TAPE She's going to love you, Rick. She'll sink her claws deep into you.

RICK A myth... that's just a myth.

RICK takes the tape player and fast forwards it.

TAPE You can't escape her, Rick.

RICK takes the tape out of the machine. The tape doesn't stop.

She's everywhere.

The image of the Ching-Shih flashes on the mirror RICK has been using. RICK smashes the tape recorder on to the ground, breaking it. There is silence. Then a muddy, thick White Noise. RICK covers his ears. Static. Then silence. RICK uncovers his ears. They are bleeding.

Scene Eight

Present. MIKE is sleeping. RICK comes into MIKE's room.

RICK Mike. Mike wake up!

MIKE *(asleep)* Get the dog whistle!

RICK Mike, it's Rick.

MIKE *(still asleep)* Bumblebee, you're the best.

RICK Mike!

MIKE sits bolt upright, screaming.

Shhh... Mike, it's just Rick.

MIKE stares at him, stone-faced now. The Book lies open.

MIKE Rick.

RICK	I'm here for an update, Mike. Have you been keeping track of me?
	Beat.
	I can't sleep, Mike. I have these dreams, these…. This woman. And me…
	It's been a fast rise to the top, Mikey. I'm starting my own firm, getting married to Tasmin, I'll be on the cover of *Profit* magazine soon… life's good. But I'm losing track, Mike. My baselines are fluctuating. Something you said about alcohol and drugs, but I can't remember which one to take first. Whatever, not important. I just need some information. You're my emergency recorder, Mike, you haven't forgotten that, have you? *(MIKE shakes his head.)* *Book*'s coming along well, then? Read me a chapter, tell me how it goes.
	Silence. Restlessness.
	I can't sleep. I need… tell me a story. About anything.
MIKE	Rick I—
RICK	I can't remember where I left off. What's the score, Mike? What have I been up to? Name, age, status, you remember… open up that black box…
MIKE	Uh… Rick Wong. 26. Formerly of Jones & Lavoie International, now heading up Richard T. Wong & Associates. Toronto's home base.
RICK	Great. Any notes?
MIKE	Notes?
RICK	Notes, you always included notes before.
MIKE	Well… there's one.
RICK	Shoot.
MIKE	You're dead, Rick. You were found yesterday morning at your condominium, a… a mirror in your chest. Through the heart. Dead.
RICK	*(pause)* Anything else?

MIKE	Did you hear me?
RICK	Is there anything else?
MIKE	No. Nothing.
RICK	Death's a state of mind, Mike. Don't you be concerned about death. Your own, maybe, but not mine.
MIKE	Sure. Okay.
RICK	*(checks his watch)* Gotta go, Mikey. Thanks for the update.
MIKE	Rick. Stay for a bit. Talk.
RICK	No time. But thanks for the offer. *(confidingly)* I always did like you best, Chao. Don't worry. I'll see you around.

> *RICK disappears. MIKE reaches out for where he used to be. Nothing. Not even air. Slowly, he begins to cry.*

ACT FOUR: THE BAD TIMES™: *In which they are undone*

Scene One

DAVE is doing a presentation. He is Reverend Jesse Jackson-ized in his exuberance. Slides are black and white until otherwise noted.

DAVE Chink. Slope. Pinko commie gook China-Boy.

AUDIENCE Mmmhmm...

DAVE Yelled from pick-up trucks, written on bathroom walls, insinuated in sideways looks from co-workers, bystanders, onlookers.

AUDIENCE Mmmhmm....

DAVE And who says 'em?! Who yells 'em? Who's driving the pick-up, writing on the walls? Who?

AUDIENCE White people!

DAVE White people. The pig-mentally challenged. The gwailo.

AUDIENCE Amen.

DAVE And do we take it? Do we sit idly by and let these words assault us? Degrade us? Bring us down? *(pause)* Yes we do! We take it. With our deference. We take it. With our chinky eyes turned downwards. We take it. With our silence, brothers and sisters, like a whore on a Sunday, we *take it.*

AUDIENCE Mmhmm...

DAVE Well I say no more! No more will we be silent!

SLIDE: A redneck teenager drinking a beer.

This White boy went to my high school. He told me he was going to kick my ass if I didn't give him my lunch money. Said I should go back to China where I belong. Did I take it? Did I lay down and let this skinny White boy get away with his vicious attack on my people? No. I did not.

AUDIENCE   Amen.

DAVE   I called the PTA. I called the AAWA. I called the ACPPA. And I said *no* to discrimination. I said *no* to racialization. I said *no* to patronization. I said *no* to artificial insemination. Just 'cause I was on a roll.

AUDIENCE   Hallelujah.

> *SLIDE: A family of White people.*

DAVE   His family got involved. They took me to court. They said I should sit down and *take it*. Why?

> *SLIDE: The graduating class of U of W.*

'Cause everyone else did. Every single one of those Chinamen sat down and *took it*.

> *SLIDE: JEANETTE and DAVE.*

Even my own girlfriend, who I loved and supported.

> *SLIDE: JEANETTE on the back of a White guy's Harley.*

Took it from the White Man. *(pause)* But this did not affect me. This did not bring me down. NO!

AUDIENCE   No!

> *SLIDE: DAVE's family at a Chinese restaurant.*

DAVE   My family taught me principles. They taught me values.

AUDIENCE   Mmmhmmm.

> *SLIDE: DAVE in his parents' arms.*

DAVE   They'd never... never...

> *The slides change now. They are in full colour, and are like the photographs taken at crime scenes or hospitals. Abuse. A young boy's chest, bruised and battered. Images come faster and faster, his face cut and black eyes and blood. The pictures are paper-clipped to medical charts, marked with pen circling the affected areas.*

Never let anything happen. Not to their son, to their…. They loved me.

Beat.

Amen.

Scene Two

SHEL and Kathy in Tim Hortons. They're breaking up. Kathy isn't necessarily present.

SHEL Double chocolate or glazed?

Beat.

I like the cake quality of the double chocolate, but the sugar of glazed is very enticing.

Beat.

We should break up. I mean, think about it rationally, things just aren't working out the way we planned. We had a great time, but now it's time to move on with our lives. For you.

Beat.

Look: The distance; check. The time commitment; check. The expenses; double check. At a purely logical, pro vs. con level, this relationship doesn't work. That's the size of it. I guess… there's just not much more to say.

Beat.

Kathy…

Beat.

I'm just trying to keep a level head over this. I was in love with you. I still love you. But things can't work out between us. It's too hard. And, frankly, I'm through with trying.

He checks his watch.

The bus to campus leaves in six minutes. You need to catch it if you don't want to be late for classes today. *(pause)* You were really great, Kath. Thanks for everything. *(He looks away, indicating the conversation is over.)*

> *After a moment.*

Whatever happened to Shel the nice guy?

> *Beat.*

Check your messages.

> *SHEL stares ahead. He tries to eat his doughnut, but his hand is suddenly shaking. He crashes.*

And so it begins.

Scene Three

> *MIKE is sleeping. He is awakened by a voice calling his name.*

VOICE   Paging Dr. Chao. Paging Dr. Michael Chao.

MIKE   Not again...

VOICE   Dr. Chao, shall I prep you for surgery?

MIKE   I'm sleeping...

VOICE   No time for sleeping, Doctor. Early bird gets the metaphor!

> *He gets up and puts his scrubs on. The Boys (including RICK) are all doctors, and are standing over the patient, concealing him from MIKE.*

Who's the patient?

RICK   First of all, Dr. Chao, I'd just like to tell you I'm a big fan.

ALL   Me too!

MIKE   Thank you, no autographs please.

SHEL   Damn it! *(He crumples up an 8x10 of MIKE and throws it away.)*

MIKE	Is the patient prepped?
LUKE	Yes, but before you look… we should warn you… you know them.
MIKE	Oh my God! Who is it? My best friend? My sister?… Not my cat?!?

> *They step aside to reveal* The Book, *tattered and shredded.*

	Sweet mother of…. *The Book!*
RICK	Doctor, control yourself!
MIKE	Quick, check the pressure and get started on a drip, I need a 15 blade, sutures and some Wite-Out.

> *They operate.*

DAVE	BP's 132 over 80.
SHEL	Pulse 110.
LUKE	We've got looseleaf, gimme more suction!
RICK	What are sutures?
MIKE	Clamp!
SHEL	Clamp.
MIKE	Grip here, now pull—

> *SHEL pulls out a bloody sheet of paper. Everyone stops. Pause.*

DAVE	Well that can't be good.
MIKE	What is it?
SHEL	A rejection letter. From a poetry contest.
LUKE	Hemorrhaging!

> *MIKE continues to explore inside the book.*

MIKE	There's more!

> *He pulls out several more sheets of paper and hands them around.*

RICK	Rejected by *Maclean's. Canadian Writer's Journal.*

SHEL	*Harper's Bazaar. The New Yorker.*
DAVE	*Penthouse Letters.*
LUKE	This one says: "Don't quit your day job. *(pause)* Unless writing is your day job, then please quit."
MIKE	*(to* The Book*)* Hang in there, dammit!
	He pulls out a larger sheet of paper and LUKE reads it.
RICK	Another rejection, doctor?
LUKE	*(reading)* Dear Mi-koh, congratulations on getting into medical school. We are so very happy for you. We love you, Mi-koh! Love, Mama.
	The doctors become MIKE's mother, except RICK, who monitors The Book.
ALL	Oh, Mi-koh! We love you!
MIKE	Oh no. No, wake up… please wake up!
	He doesn't wake up. The Boys surround him in a suffocating group hug, chanting "We love you!"
	Wake up!
	RICK hovers over The Book, *poking it a few times. He is sullen.*
RICK	He's dead, Jim.

Scene Four

RICK	Testing. Toast… toast… toast. Baseline Video number… number…. Number 1. Baseline Video number 1. Date is Saturday, January 1st, 2172, time 12:00am midnight. Hi, Rick. You handsome devil you.
	He switches intermittently between Cantonese and English. Italics in this scene are Cantonese.
	They come for me fast… very fast… fucking seraphs with their fucking wings beating… I fear I am… I have fear… I never used to fear anything… now, now because of you,

because of... *it's in my blood because of you. You* weakling, you pussy, you *bred it into me, you* the father is weak, but the son... *the son is supposed to be* strong, should be so strong, but you... I hate you. *You bred me to be weak to have fear* now *at the worst moment.* Need more...

What am I doing? *What the fuck am I doing?* This isn't right. Stop. Rewind. *Go back to the beginning.* I didn't listen. I never listened.

He takes more pills and drowns them in alcohol.

I've been warned. I have received a warning. *From the best doctor I ever knew. He told me* the pills and the alcohol, *I'm supposed to* mix *them, but how? I don't remember.* Which *comes* first? *And now I need courage, I need salvation, and* where the fuck are you guys?

Someone tell me.

Scene Five

Lights. Music. LUKE is at a rave. He is dancing fluidly, almost furiously. The music reaches a climax, then begins to fade out.

LUKE is worried. Silence encroaches. He keeps dancing. The volume bounces up slightly, encouraging him. He dances. The music again fades. LUKE tries to get it back by dancing harder, faster, more kinetic. The music continues to fade. LUKE is sweating. His legs are burning. He is pushing himself.

The music is gone completely. LUKE still dances. He can barely stand, but he continues.

There is now no sound but his own laboured breathing. Spent, he collapses on the floor.

Scene Six

DAVE is alone.

DAVE   **Racial Incident Log. Incident: #432.**

Beat.

Racial Incident Log. Incident: #649.

Beat.

Racial Incident Log. Incident: #844.

Beat, he is losing control.

Incident: #980.

Beat.

Incident: #1245.

Beat.

#4204

#9279, #14201, #67485...

Beat. Beat. Beat.

Notes: I woke up last night and I was covered in blood. There was broken glass everywhere, and my knuckles were... raw. I don't remember how I got there, or why...

I woke up last night and I was covered in blood. Fucked up thing is: not a drop of it was mine.

Beat.

Grade: ... I don't know.

Beat.

Comments: ...

Beat. He lights a cigarette.

Good job, soldier. For that, you get a Coke.

Beat. He smiles, rueful and sad.

Scene Seven

All five Boys are at the Bomb Shelter. They are inebriated, but lucid… and miserable. DAVE is smoking next to MIKE.

MIKE   Dave, can you not blow smoke in my face, it's fucking obnoxious.

DAVE   Sure, would you mind bitching and whining downwind from *me*? I'm getting second-hand suicidal tendencies.

LUKE   Shut up and smoke somewhere else, it's annoying both of us.

DAVE   Why do you always…? Look, pretend this is school, and just give up.

LUKE   I didn't *give up*. I just… I need time to figure out what I want in life.

RICK   You'll be dead before you figure that out.

They look at him.

Just sayin' is all…

LUKE   Oh, I'm sorry Rick – not all of us take the fast track to World Domination. Some people actually want to facilitate *real change*.

RICK   And a psychology degree was going to do that? If you can't even finish *that*, you're fucking hopeless.

MIKE   And what's your plan, Rick?

RICK   Fortune and glory, kid. Fortune and glory.

DAVE   Just like an FOB.

RICK   Shut your fucking mouth.

SHEL   *(ever the peacemaker)* Never mind them, I hate those Chinese Christians, they're always making me feel guilty about going to church and stuff.

MIKE   When was the last time you were in church Shel?

SHEL   I'd rather not say.

LUKE	You see; it's all stereotypes. The world's full of them so get over it! What pisses me off are those hardcore Asian American activists. Every time a movie or a sitcom or a Taco Bell commercial comes on without an Asian presence, they get all wound up and make it out to be the biggest crime since Martin Luther King Jr. was shot.
DAVE	Now who's stereotyping?
LUKE	Oh shut-up.
MIKE	Guys, we're all Chinese right? We're all Asian. We're brothers. Sticking together is vitally important for our political solidarity...
RICK	Would you guys shut up already! There is no political solidarity.
MIKE	Of course there is—
RICK	No, there isn't. And the more you fucking whine and cry about it, the more hopeless the case becomes. The reason, the *real* reason the Asian race, as a people, as a movement, have not progressed forward... is motherfuckers just – like – you.
LUKE	Well if heartless bastards like you would take two seconds to actually care about something other than yourselves we'd actually get somewhere!
RICK	You're calling *me* heartless? That's rich. Seen *your* heart lately, pussy?
DAVE	Lay off him, Rick. He's just confused.
LUKE	Fuck off, Dave, you're the last person I want coming to my defence.
DAVE	Now what the hell is that supposed to mean?
LUKE	It means you should deal with your own goddamn problems before you start in on solving mine.
DAVE	Don't you dare lay your pop-psychology on me!
LUKE	Then don't lay your frustrations and your pathetic inadequacies on me!
SHEL	Guys—

DAVE	Jeeeeezus Christ! You don't just lay pop-psychology! You *are* pop-psychology!
LUKE	And you're fucking substance right? Render unto me a fucking break you racist, misogynistic child!
DAVE	I'm a child? You bounce around in a fisherman's cap, waving glowsticks in the air for hours, and *I'm* the child?
RICK	Lover's quarrel?
DAVE	Shut the fuck up.
RICK	You talk to me like that? You blue-collar piece of shit, with your small-town baggage—
DAVE	It's a thin fucking line you're walking, son.
SHEL	Okay, guys, we've *all* had a lot to drink… let's just calm down, lower our voices…
LUKE	Shut up, Shel.
SHEL	Fuck! I'm so fucking tired of everyone telling me to shut up! Just because I'm the well-adjusted one out of all of us, that doesn't invalidate what I say!
DAVE	I'm sorry? *You're* well adjusted?
SHEL	I am.
LUKE	If you call putting all your self-respect into a futile Quest "well-adjusted," then yah, you're a fucking pillar.
SHEL	And who says it's futile?
LUKE	We *all* think it's futile, Shel.
DAVE	And you're one to talk?
MIKE	Rick, let them be, please!
RICK	Shel, say it's not your fault.
SHEL	It's not my fault you guys are all embittered and cynical.
MIKE	Shel, stop. Can't you see what—
SHEL	Shut up, Mike.
RICK	Now Dave tells Mike not to start, and Luke calls Shel deluded.

Simultaneously:

LUKE   You're deluded, Shel! Christ, if we were on the *Titanic* you'd be playing all the way down.

DAVE   Don't *you* start, Mike, if we listened to you, the five of us'd all be strung up in our closets.

RICK   Everybody now!

Simultaneously:

Shel, call him on faith. Dave, they're all self righteous pricks. Luke, call them self-absorbed. Mike, shut the fuck up!

SHEL   At least I've got the courage to have faith in something. I'm surprised you even make it out your door in the morning, coward.

MIKE   Goddamnit, Rick, I've fucking had it with this mindshifting bullshit! Guys, please stop, it's him, it's Rick he's—

DAVE   Fucking hell, where do you self-righteous pricks get off? You're all fucking delusional. It's pathetic.

LUKE   You guys are so self-absorbed with your First World problems and fake plastic trees, I'm fucking sick and tired of it!

MIKE   *Everyone shut the fuck up!!!*

Silence.

RICK   This should be good.

MIKE   The fuck's the matter with you? Pay attention to me, now. What are you if not one of us? You self-righteous prick. Fucking junkie, laying this moral highground shit, *(in Cantonese) you can't suck the life from them, I won't let you, you fucking Ching-Shih!*

        RICK punches MIKE in the face. He falls back. The Boys are silent. RICK is at once horrified/intoxicated/ relieved. He staggers backwards, towards the door.

RICK   You fucking cunts deserve each other.

He staggers out the door, and as he closes it, the chimes are similar to the pealing bells from the prologue.

Shift. Years later. MIKE's cell phone rings, he answers.

MIKE   Hello?

He listens for a second. Stunned, he walks over to where RICK had been standing, and looks at all The Boys.

Guys. *(He hangs up the phone.)* It's Rick. *(pause)* Rick's dead.

LUKE   And so it begins.

The Boys stare at each other in silence. Slowly, Mental White Noise starts to fill the room. Static electric snow grows out of all of them. At the very last second, it is all transferred to MIKE, who doubles over in pain. He coughs up blood.

Blackout.

Intermission.

ACT FIVE: PYLOXIDIN™: *In which they are released*

Scene One

MIKE is in his study lab. RICK comes in.

MIKE   Rick.

RICK   Mikey.

     Beat.

MIKE   Been a while.

RICK   A year, I guess.

MIKE   More than that.

RICK   Maybe. A lot's happened.

MIKE   So I've heard. *(RICK raises an eyebrow.)* Caught your name on the business report on 680 News. You're starting your own firm.

RICK   Started. Furniture came in Thursday.

MIKE   Congratulations.

RICK   Yeah.

     Pause.

     I own a condominium.

     Pause.

MIKE   The whole thing, or just a unit?

RICK   Penthouse.

MIKE   That's… that's great.

RICK   Yah, it is.

     Pause.

     I drive a BMW.

MIKE   What are you doing here, Rick?

RICK   Don't get like that about it.

MIKE	You drove a BMW at school too, Rick. It was impressive then, I'm sure it's just as impressive now.
RICK	It is.
MIKE	I'm sure.
RICK	Forget it. You don't understand.

> *Beat.*

MIKE	So what are you doing here?
RICK	Can't a guy come back to see an old friend?
MIKE	Sure he can. But you're not that guy.
RICK	Pyloxidin…
MIKE	Rick…
RICK	I just need a little more. Just a little. The new office, and Tasmin is… things are a little stressful.
MIKE	I can't help.
RICK	C'mon Mikey, I just need a little prescription, they don't care where it comes from. My regular guy, he cut… he's out of town, and I can't… c'mon, Mike.
MIKE	You should leave.

> *Beat.*

RICK	Well. Guess that's that.
MIKE	I can't. I'm not—
RICK	So, how's the writing coming?
MIKE	Why do you always ask me that?
RICK	I'm interested.

> *Pause.*

MIKE	It's not about you. *The Book*, I mean. It's not.
RICK	Sure it isn't.
MIKE	That's the only reason you care, isn't it? Because you think you're in here. That this is your gospel according to Mike. Isn't it?

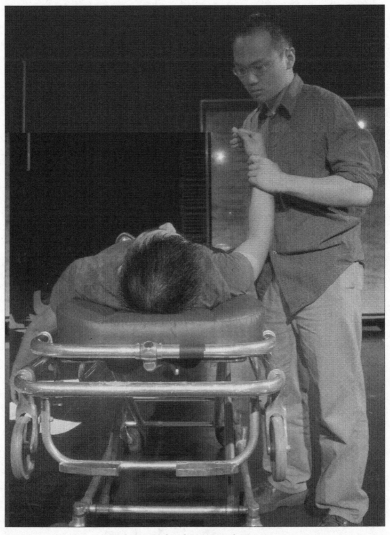

l to r: Richard Lee, Derek Kwan
photo by Guy Bertrand

Pause.

RICK   What are you going to do if everything stays the same, Mike? What's going to happen if nothing changes?

MIKE   I don't know.

RICK	That's the easiest answer there is. You, the rest of The Boys... "I don't know." Like it was some kinda motto. The boyscouts had "always be prepared," you guys had "I don't know."

    Beat.

MIKE	Rick, in the last year or... whatever it's been... did you ever think about us? Even once? Me. The Boys. Any of us?
RICK	Sure. Sure I did. I... but you don't understand, the stresses of... of, um... *(Shift, the Ching-Shih floats past the door.)* Fuck! She's here! The Ching-Shih. She's here and she can smell the fear in my blood! *(Shift, she's gone.)* Mike?
MIKE	What's happening?
RICK	I'm mindshifting. There's not much time. I need... *(shift)* Five years from now, you're playing street hockey with Dave and Luke. Shel's not there, he's.... You're drinking beer and laughing and talking about old times. Dave got promoted and Luke has a real job. It's awful. I'm there too but no one sees me. No one but you. *(shift)*
MIKE	Rick, we need to get you to a hospital.
RICK	No hospitals! Just... find ou...

    He is gripped with pain. He coughs up blood.

MIKE	Jesus... I'm calling an ambulance.
RICK	No! No, they'll... they study you, Mike. They'll find my kryptonite... I'll run. I'll run and fucking hide and you'll never find me until the light comes flooding in and then I'll just turn to dust, Mike. I'll turn to dust, to ash, to fucking ashes... *(He scrambles out the door.)*
MIKE	Rick, wait!

    RICK halts at the door.

    In case this... I've missed you.

    RICK smiles.

RICK	Someone has to.

Scene Two

RICK is filming a Baseline Video.

RICK   It's changed. I can feel it in my veins, the blood. It used to ebb and flow, but now it's just stopped. It stopped, and I'm cold. I've never felt anything like this. No bottle, no pill feels like this. I love it. I need more.

He takes a drink, but spits out blood all over his camera, his television. He is drinking blood from 40oz bottles.

Something is wrong with me. There is something wrong with me. Something with me is very wrong. Very very wrong. Jesus I need a drink. I need to recover I need a womb. I need... rice.

He stands and yells "Give me a bowl of rice" in Cantonese.

Scene Three

The Boys are all in reflective states. RICK walks amongst them, unseen.

DAVE is smoking a cigarette, hunched over his computer, staring blankly at the screen. SHEL is sitting under his kitchen table, cradling his cell phone like a sick child. LUKE is in the 808 State flipping absent-mindedly through CDs. MIKE is trying to write. He breaks pencil after pencil, crumples paper after paper.

RICK watches them. They are all thinking about him. Maybe they just don't know it.

Simultaneously: DAVE's IM notification beeps. SHEL's cell phone rings. There's a knock at LUKE's door. A breeze blows the crumpled paper around MIKE's room.

> *Simultaneously: DAVE types a message. SHEL answers his phone. LUKE walks to the door. MIKE goes to the window.*

ALL Hello?

> *There is no answer.*

> *RICK stands among them. He watches them look around, then go back to what they'd been distracting themselves with. A family picture is taken.*

> *RICK disappears.*

Scene Four

> *DAVE is in a chair, in an interrogation room. It is shortly after RICK's death. He is being grilled by two cops, sitting across from him.*

COP 1 Name?

DAVE David Lowe.

COP 1 How do you spell that?

DAVE D-a-v-i-d. L-o-w-e.

COP 2 E?

DAVE That's what I said.

COP 2 Low with an E?

DAVE There a problem with that?

COP 1 No problem.

COP 2 Just not how you spell things.

DAVE Not how *White people* spell things, you mean.

COP 1 Take it easy, son.

DAVE Bitch, please.

COP 2 Just relax. You people are so sensitive.

DAVE You people?

COP 1   All right, stop it! *(to other cop)* Take it easy, his friend just died.

> *Shift. SHEL is being interrogated.*

COP 2   You want to state your name for the record.

SHEL   Yes, officer. Sheldon Kwan, officer.

COP 2   Kwan?

SHEL   Officer, yes, officer.

COP 1   Kwan, do you know where you were the night of the thirteenth?

SHEL   Officer, yes I do. *(pause)* Officer.

COP 1   Where were you, exactly?

SHEL   Officer, I was at the Madison Pub. 2nd floor, 14 Madison Ave. *(pause)* 416-927-1722.

COP 2   You know the phone number?

SHEL   We go there a lot, Officer.

> *Shift. LUKE's interrogation.*

COP 1   We?

LUKE   The Boys.

COP 2   "The Boys." Are you referring to yourself, Mr. Kwan, Mr. Lowe and Mr. Chao?

LUKE   Yup.

COP 2   But not Mr. Wong?

LUKE   Nope.

COP 1   Do you know where Mr. Wong was that evening?

LUKE   Nope.

COP 2   Are you aware Mr. Wong was found dead the following morning?

LUKE   *(pause)* Yup.

COP 1   Is there anything you'd like to tell us about that?

l to r: Insurp Choi, Dale Yim, Derek Kwan, Richard Lee, David Yee
photo by Guy Bertrand

LUKE	Nope.

> *Shift. DAVE's interrogation.*

COP 1	Do you or anyone you know have any bad blood with Mr. Wong?
DAVE	Rick. Could you just… call him Rick.
COP 1	Okay. Anyone you know have bad blood with… Rick?
DAVE	Lotta people.
COP 2	Including you?

> *DAVE is silent.*

COP 2	Isn't it true the two of you were involved in a scuffle a few years ago at the University of Waterloo?
DAVE	No scuffle. The mother-of-all-arguments, yah, but… look: we were drunk, he got pissed off, punched Mikey and rode off into the sunset like Butch Cassidy.

COP 2	Interesting analogy. Considering Butch Cassidy was later killed.
COP 1	So you were pretty angry with Mr.... with Rick?
DAVE	Yeah, but... no, not enough to... hey, the fuck is this?
COP 2	We got a dead body and four suspects whose only alibis are each other. So start talking, fuckbag!
	Pause.
DAVE	Are you pissed off 'cause you couldn't get a date to the Policeman's Ball?
COP 2	No, smartass. Ontario Provincial Police Officers don't have any Balls.
	Beat. DAVE snickers.
	You son of a—
	Shift. SHEL's interrogation.
SHEL	Officer, I don't think any of us had anything to do with Rick's death.
COP 1	Do you miss him?
SHEL	What?
COP 1	He was your friend, Shel. He was there through university, when Olivia Tan broke your heart. He helped you study for—
SHEL	I know, Officer.
COP 1	But you don't miss him?
SHEL	Officer I don't see the relevance in—
COP 2	When did you see him last?
SHEL	Over a year ago, Officer. Maybe two, I don't know. Not since the mother-of-all-arguments.
COP 1	Are you sure?
SHEL	Officer, I... I don't see where—

COP 2	We obtained Mr. Wong's PDA and the lab's been through it. His schedule suggests something contrary to your story. *(pause)* Did he contact you?
	Shift. LUKE's interrogation.
LUKE	Nope.
COP 1	It says right here: "Luke, 11pm, Velvet Underground." He didn't come see you?
	LUKE is silent.
COP 2	He's gone, Luke. He's gone and you never got a chance to say goodbye. Just like your father, isn't it?
LUKE	Yup.
COP 1	So why don't you tell us what happened?
	Shift. Nightclub – The Velvet Underground. LUKE is spinning, his headphones on. RICK enters.
RICK	Luke. *(nothing)* Luke. *(nothing)* Hey Luke!
	LUKE looks over.
	Can we talk?
	LUKE motions to his headphones. Can't hear anything.
	I just wanted to… to talk a bit.
	Again, the headphones.
	I wanted to catch up, maybe… talk a bit. You're busy, I can… I can see that. Maybe later, after. Swa Tao, at 1:00, how 'bout?
	LUKE gestures around him, then to the headphones again.
	Luke I need… I've been thinking and…
	Nothing. LUKE stares straight ahead.
	Okay then. Maybe… maybe later.
	Shift. LUKE's interrogation.
COP 1	But you didn't talk to him? He needed you. He reached out for you. And you couldn't even acknowledge him?

       LUKE is breaking.

LUKE   Nope.

COP 2   So you knew he was in trouble?

LUKE   Yup.

COP 1   And did absolutely nothing.

LUKE   *(He is near tears.)* Nope.

       Shift. DAVE's interrogation.

DAVE   The fuck was I supposed to do? He calls me, he... he... I'm at work. I have a job. I have... bills, and and *responsibility*. And he, what?

COP 1   Calm down, Mr. Lowe.

DAVE   You are not pinning this on me, on... no! He calls, he says he needs my help with something. His computer has some virus or whatever the fuck, and now after years he wants me to... fuck that.

COP 2   Calm down, Dave.

DAVE   I am fucking calm! Rick Wong was not a fucking hero! He was not a martyr, he didn't die for someone else's sins, he died for... for what? I don't know! But one goddamn phone call does not a best friend make.

COP 1   Maybe he had a change of heart.

DAVE   You'd need a heart first.

       Shift. SHEL's interrogation. He is a blubbering mess.

SHEL   I should've listened to him.... He wasn't making any sense, he was just rambling about some woman that was after him... and Rick always had women after him, it wasn't out of the ordinary, he just said it and I didn't listen and I should have listened but my bus was there and it was cold and I just wanted to go home. I didn't know he sought me out, that he came for me, for... he said that he missed us, that he missed us all so much and I didn't listen, I stopped listening because it was years ago and all of us had moved on and I didn't want to know it was wrong it was wrong it was wrong… *(He keeps mumbling to himself.)*

COP 1   *(to COP 2)* Are you happy now?

COP 2   I didn't say anything! I just asked if he wanted a cup of coffee.

SHEL   I'm sorry, Rick… I'm sorry I'm so sorry, I missed you too. We all missed you we all… it's my fault. It's all my fault…

        Pause.

     Am I going to jail?

Scene Five

RICK is filming his last Baseline Video. The image is blurry. He is becoming the Ching-Shih, and he no longer has a reflection.

RICK   I am sitting in a penthouse suite, surrounded by 40mg doses of hope and overturned bottles of love. The suit I am wearing cost two thousand dollars. I can't tell you what my name is, but I know it was two thousand dollars. What the fuck does that mean?

     I don't recognize this place. I know it's mine, but I don't… everything's so fucking foreign. Who left me here? Who… *(shift)* Mike… where was I just now? Don't make me go back. I don't want to go back…

        There is a sound just past his peripheral vision. He spins around.

     Fuck. No time, not enough…

        He trails off as the sound of voices come closer.

VOICE   Paging Dr. Chao. Paging Dr. Michael Chao.

RICK   The fuck is that?

MIKE   I'm sleeping…

VOICE	No time for sleeping, Doctor. This man needs your urgent attention!

> *The Boys enter, without MIKE, and tie RICK down to the bed.*

RICK	Let go of me! Let—

> *They anaesthetize him. He passes out. MIKE enters.*

MIKE	Who's the patient?
LUKE	He's the one on the bed.
MIKE	Good. What's wrong with him?
SHEL	That's why we called you, Dr. Chao. We *just don't know!*

> *MIKE surveys RICK. He hems and haws.*

MIKE	Has he been through radiology?
SHEL	Normal.
MIKE	Cardiology?
LUKE	Normal.
MIKE	Scientology?
DAVE	Normal.
MIKE	Hmm…

> *He pokes and prods RICK.*

Doctors.

ALL 3	Yes?
MIKE	This man has a large mirror stuck in his chest.

> *Pause.*

DAVE	Goddammit, that's why you're the best.
MIKE	Remove the mirror, let's see what else is inside.

> *They remove the mirror and begin digging around in RICK's chest. They pull out various items, one by one.*

Inventory.

LUKE	Gucci money clip.

SHEL	Prescription drugs.
DAVE	Polaroid photo.
MIKE	Of?
DAVE	Indeterminable. Maybe someone's feet?
MIKE	That can't be right. Next.
LUKE	BMW, 3-Series Coupe.
SHEL	Lakefront condo. *(A price tag reading $530,000 hangs off it.)*
DAVE	Berlitz tape.
	They root around some more.
LUKE	He's empty, Doc.
MIKE	Empty?
DAVE	*(sticks his head in RICK's chest)* Nothing else in here.
SHEL	The condo took up a lot of room.
LUKE	How should we proceed, doctor?
MIKE	Well… in my expert medical opinion… *(pause)* He's dead. What else can we do?
LUKE	Can't save 'em all.
MIKE	You certainly can't. *(pause)* Let's get drunk.
	They all cheer and start to leave. RICK sits bolt upright, awake.
RICK	Mike!

Scene Six

RICK is still filming his last Baseline Video.

RICK	Baseline Video number 324. If you are watching this, it means I'm dead. I've been killed. And there's a murderer on the loose. Among you. I tried to stop but this killer is relentless. Won't stop. Never stop. Not until I'm dead. I…

He stops, looking to his side.

Did you hear that? Shit.

He takes a swig of alcohol.

Getting closer. I make this video in preparation for what I know my fate is. The price I have to pay for what I've become. *(in Cantonese) The beast comes and it smells like success and fast cars.* I'm going to pay.

We all pay.

I make this video because I need you to do something for me. Find Michael Chao.

Scene Seven

The boys are at RICK's funeral. They are standing over RICK's body.

SHEL	So what do we do?
LUKE	Just carry him out.
DAVE	Lift with the legs.
MIKE	That's good advice.
SHEL	And then we what?
DAVE	Hearse.
LUKE	Cemetery.
MIKE	Crying, probably.
DAVE	Not me.
LUKE	His mother.
MIKE	Girlfriend. What's her name?
SHEL	Tasmin.
MIKE	She hasn't stopped.
LUKE	Then a eulogy.

MIKE	That's my whale.

        DAVE looks at MIKE questioningly.

	Moby Dick.
LUKE	Then we go home.
DAVE	I thought Moby Dick was a shark.
SHEL	Just like that?
MIKE	Moby Dick was a whale.
LUKE	Just like that.
DAVE	I think it was a shark.
MIKE	What's the problem, Shel?
SHEL	Just like that? We move on with our… what?
LUKE	Jaws was a shark.
DAVE	I gotta go back to work after this.
MIKE	I've got MCAT cribs on the back of the eulogy notes.
SHEL	I…. It just doesn't seem right.
DAVE	No, it doesn't. *(to LUKE)* You're sure?
SHEL	We carry him out?
LUKE	Yah. Jaws.
SHEL	But we carry him out?
LUKE	That too.
MIKE	He's got places to go.
LUKE	Schedule to keep.
DAVE	Is it too soon for irony?
SHEL	And then we do what?
LUKE	I gotta hand out resumes.
DAVE	They make resumes for what you do?
MIKE	Do you think they'll be listening?
LUKE/DAVE	You'll be fine.

SHEL/MIKE	I don't know about that.
DAVE	It's just a eulogy.
SHEL	And then we do what?
MIKE	I'm scared.
LUKE	Stop asking that.
DAVE	We're all scared.

       Pause.

MIKE	What's with his face?
SHEL	I can't do it.
MIKE	It's different, like.
SHEL	I'll drop him, or tip it over…
LUKE	No you won't.
MIKE	Not what I expected.
DAVE	It's been a while. Since we've seen him, like.
MIKE	No, it's… not that long.
LUKE	Years, hasn't it?
MIKE	The other week.

       Pause.

SHEL	It's a lot of weight.
DAVE	You didn't mention—
MIKE	No.
SHEL	To carry, I mean.
MIKE	And he looked different then, but… more now.
LUKE	You should've said something.
SHEL	Why did they ask us?
MIKE	I don't know.
DAVE	S'almost rush hour. I should email, maybe.
LUKE	Just one of those days.

MIKE	Maybe 'cause he would've…
LUKE	Everything's running late.
MIKE	…I don't know.

Pause.

SHEL	He's not smiling.
MIKE	Hm?
DAVE	Jaws was the shark.
SHEL	He was always smiling.
LUKE	That's it, isn't it?
MIKE	Told you.
SHEL	S'why he looks different.
MIKE	He should be smiling.

Pause. A bell tolls.

I think that's it.

They stand for a long time in silence.

Scene Eight

RICK rises from the dead. The other boys are unaware of him, even as he jumps out of his coffin to confront MIKE. They are at once in the cemetery and RICK's condominium.

RICK	Mike.

MIKE spins around and falls.

MIKE	Jesus!
RICK	No, just me.
MIKE	Rick.
RICK	Did you finish it?
MIKE	Finish what?

RICK	*The Book.*
MIKE	Finish… no. Rick, I never started.
RICK	*(He is crestfallen.)* All this time…
MIKE	Rick, I—
RICK	What the fuck have you been doing?!? This…

> *He gathers up sheets of paper that are lying on the floor of his condo, and throws them at MIKE.*

What the fuck is this, then? Huh? What is it that you haven't started, Michael?

> *He reads the papers, excerpts of MIKE's book.*

"He fears sunlight. It lapses behind drawn curtains in his bedroom. He is becoming what he fears the most…"

MIKE	Where did you get that?
RICK	Mikey, you have to finish it. Because you… you kept track of me, didn't you? My emergency recorder…
MIKE	No. I'm… I'm a doctor.
RICK	My black box.
MIKE	Things are different.
RICK	You have to write it. I'm counting on you—
MIKE	Stop it! I am so fucking sick of people telling me what to do! "Be a doctor, Michael," "Write *The Book*, Michael," "Don't put that in your mouth, Michael." What about *you*, huh?
RICK	What—
MIKE	You are… were… was…
RICK	Tenses aren't important.
MIKE	A fucking *mistake*! I gave you—
RICK	What?
MIKE	Everything! Everything I should have been doing, everything I could have done, and it's lost. It was aborted by you. It was all a mistake. You're an error. A regret.

	Fixing your cuts and bruises; remembering your fucking name for you... *(beat)* I could have been something.
RICK	And what's that?
MIKE	I... I don't know.
RICK	That's right. You don't know. *(He gestures to The Boys.)* They don't know. What happens if nothing changes, Mike? I can tell you. I've been there. Dave's health gets worse. Stress from too much work and too many cigarettes. He dies at 32. Luke gives up deejaying and gets a job as a data entry clerk, miserable bastard. He tries to kill himself three times before he gets it right. Shel... our Shel... he had the brightest future. The One was waiting for him in Hong Kong, y'know that? But he never went. He gives up and settles down with someone he doesn't love. She has an affair, and our Shel dies of a broken heart.
MIKE	You're lying...
RICK	You have to tell them. Tell them there's more out there. Let my story be an example for them. Let my life teach them their dreams are possible. They're your friends, Mikey, you can't let them all die alone, unsatisfied... hollow. This Banana Boy shit—this non-identity—won't get them anywhere.
MIKE	You were one of us, Rick.
RICK	Stop saying that! I was better! I was more! I was a fucking inspiration! Write that down, tell them that!
MIKE	I've been lying for you your whole life, Rick.

RICK punches MIKE in the mouth.

| **RICK** | You failure. You fraud. |

He kicks him in the head.

You weak pussy!

He punches him in the stomach.

Paging Doctor Chao, Doctor Michael Chao!

He breaks his wrist.

Why don't they miss me? Why don't…. Why doesn't anyone care?!?

He kicks him in the ribs.

Write it, Mike. Give them some hope, give them…

He crushes his throat.

Write it or they're all going to die. And you'll be alone.

MIKE is choking. RICK releases him, and he gasps for air.

I'm dead, Mike. But at least I know who I am.

MIKE picks up a sheet of paper from the floor. He takes a broken pencil out of his shirt pocket. He writes.

MIKE	Four of them enter a long, narrow room, carrying a load on their shoulders.
RICK	**Name:** Richard Wong.
MIKE	They've come to answer one last question before leaving this place and going separate ways.
RICK	**Age:** 26.
MIKE	So they say goodbye;
RICK	Status—
MIKE	Not to the addict—
RICK	—Status…
MIKE	—or to the vampire—
RICK	—Status…
MIKE	—or to the senior consultant. They put their friend to rest. Their brother. Knowing he was one of them…

RICK's skin starts to burn.

They are one less in number…

RICK	What's happening?

MIKE   They are one step ahead. They can stop searching and walk on solid ground. They've put their friend to rest. And now it's their turn.

RICK begins to shift. The television in his condominium turns on by itself and starts to play his last Baseline Video.

RICK   **Name:** Richard Wong... age 26... status... status... fucking status...

MIKE rejoins the funeral. The boys begin carrying RICK's empty coffin to his grave.

MIKE   The Romantic, The Cynic, The Lost Soul and The Doctor. They stand up. They loosen the curtains. Light floods in, and lays bare every broken thing, every stitch and scar. But at least they're at the window. At least they're in the light.

RICK   Mike?

MIKE   The Doctor steps forward and removes his coat. He's tired of fixing people. He's tired of the lies and malpractice. He's going to tell the truth.

RICK   I trusted you!

MIKE   He is the writer. He is the poet. He is the prophet. He is the fighter.

RICK   Where was I just now? Don't make me go back there... don't make me go back!

MIKE   He is the one who stands up and raises his voice. It cracks and it trembles, but he raises it anyway. Because, sooner or later, someone has to.

RICK   Stop. Rewind.

Shift. RICK is reliving the last moments of his life.

Baseline Video number... number...

MIKE   Because everyone has a place in this world. It's about time they found theirs.

RICK yells "give me a bowl of rice!" in Cantonese.

RICK	No fork! My life is like a game of Monopoly gone completely to hell… Boardwalk, Park Place, all the railroads – I've mortgaged them twice over – but the damn board is on this *goddamn fucking infinity loop*!
MIKE	Together again, the five of us reunited, I am presented with a truth I can not quite reconcile.
RICK	So what can you do? Work fiercely, very hard, at the risk of wasting your limited resources, never ever getting back to where everything was normal?
MIKE	I am conscious of something I have been sleeping through for years.
RICK	Or stop playing the game entirely, start someplace new, with what I've learned.
MIKE	Standing here, six feet above someone I used to know…
RICK	This is what I've learned to do. This is what I did. This is what I shall continue doing until the day I die.

        Simultaneously:

MIKE	…with tear streaked faces, trippy places, all of these beautiful lies. I am faced with this simple and singular fact:
RICK	Erased. Over. Out. Jesus I need a drink. I need to recover I need a womb. I need…
MIKE	I loved him the most.

        Shift.

RICK	So where were you when I needed you? Huh? Where were you with the beer and the hands to pick me up?

        Shift.

Stop! Rewind! Baseline Video number…. Fuck!

        Shift.

I am sitting in a penthouse suite, surrounded by 40mg doses of hope and overturned bottles of love. The suit I am wearing cost two thousand dollars. I can't tell

you what my name is, but I know it was two thousand
dollars. What the fuck does that mean?

I don't recognize this place. I know it's mine, but
I don't... everything's so fucking foreign. I need...
a drink. I need to recover I need a womb I need...

He is becoming undone.

Stop. Fucking rewind. Baseline Video number... two
thousand dollars... I need a drink. I need... I need...

RICK yells "give me a bowl of rice!" in Cantonese.

No fork! Dammit I said no fork can't you understand you
fuckin' fob – I want it all I got it all I – I – I...

*He is now staring at MIKE, through the mirror. The
mirror becomes alternately reflective and transparent,
flashing on and off. He is looking at himself, then
MIKE, then himself.*

I know you. I know you...

RICK/MIKE   *Wo ei ni.*

RICK begins to bleed.

MIKE picks up the mirror.

MIKE   Rick?

RICK looks up.

You're not paying attention.

*MIKE rams the mirror into RICK's chest. There is
a loud crash of breaking glass. Projected, in rapid
succession are images of RICK punching the mirror,
shattering it. The effect is like flip-book animation. The
images bleed red.*

RICK dies.

*Shift. The funeral. MIKE is standing over RICK's
grave, not moving.*

LUKE   Mike.

No answer.

DAVE   Mike, we should…

            Nothing.

SHEL   We should go somewhere.

DAVE   Have a beer or… twelve.

LUKE   Where we going? Mike? We're going to…

            Nothing.

            Where should we… uh…

            Pause. MIKE starts to say "I don't know," but stops himself.

MIKE   Somewhere else.

Epilogue

The Boys are now at the airport. A P.A. calls flights leaving for Hong Kong and Vancouver.

DAVE S'our flight, Shelly.

He shoulders his bag. SHEL hugs MIKE.

MIKE *(laughing)* Get off me.

SHEL I'll email you once I'm settled.

DAVE You sure you don't want to come to Hong Kong, Mikey? I'm gonna be all lonely once Shel starts work. At least tell me how to say "Where's the bar" in Cantonese.

MIKE *(says "I have a small penis" in Cantonese)* Practice that. Take care. *(They shake, and share a "man hug.")*

DAVE Later, Hippy.

LUKE Later, Bitch.

SHEL hugs LUKE.

Get off me. *(smiles)* Take care of that one, okay? *(indicating DAVE)*

SHEL Will do.

LUKE I should get to my Terminal. Mikey… *(They "man hug.")* Boys.

MIKE Not that I don't have faith in you, Luke. But if you drop out again, I'll fucking come to Vancouver and kill you myself.

LUKE You're so sentimental. I'll be fine. You'll visit?

MIKE Soon as I got the time.

DAVE Mikey, we left something with your parents.

SHEL Going away present.

LUKE I gotta jet.

SHEL Us too. C'mon honey.

Derek Kwan
photo by Guy Bertrand

DAVE   Yes dear.

> *They all start to leave, DAVE and SHEL to one side,
> LUKE to the other, leaving MIKE in the middle. The
> Boys all wave, and exit.*

> *Shift. MIKE is at home. He reaches under the bed, and
> opens a wrapped box. Inside is an old typewriter, some
> paper and a card. MIKE reads the card, and loads
> some paper into the typewriter. He stares at it. Mental
> White Noise starts filtering in. MIKE begins typing,
> and the Mental White Noise dies out.*

> *Projected, we see what he is writing:*

> *Banana Boys
> By Michael Chao
> In Loving Memory of Rick Wong*

He stops.

MIKE   And so it ends.

Pause. He types.

And so it begins...

The lights slowly fade on MIKE, as he types. The sound of the typewriter carries through into the blackout.

The end.

Leon Aureus is an actor, playwright and producer. He is the founding Artistic Director of The Gum San Theatre Company which blossomed into the fu-GEN Theatre Company (www.fu-gen.org) in 2002. *Banana Boys* is his first play and was also fu-GEN's first full production. The play's development paralleled the exciting growth of the company, neither of which would have been possible without the vision, dedication, hard work and brilliance of his fellow 'fu-GEN'ers Nina Lee Aquino, Richard Lee and David Yee. He thanks and cherishes them for being on that journey with him.

He also wrote and directed the short film "Friends Like These" and co-wrote the play *People Power* (for the Carlos Bulosan Theatre Company).

Born in Quezon City, Philippines, he immigrated to Canada at a very young age, growing up in Toronto's East End (a few blocks away from the kids of Degrassi) and the 'burbs of Mississauga – but never forgetting his roots. Well maybe a little... or even a lot. But it's that continuing path of searching and discovery that keeps him writing and creating. He currently lives in Toronto's Annex neighbourhood where the rowdy drunken college kids also keep him (up) writing and creating.